The *Really* WILD Food Guide

Food Guide

or

350+ Ways to Wok the Wild

Johnny Jumbalaya

The Really Wild Food Guide

or

350+ Ways to Wok the Wild

Johnny Jumbalaya

First published in 2002

Copyright © Johnny Jumbalaya, 2002

ISBN 0 9544158 0 9

www.countrylovers.co.uk/wildfoodjj

INTRODUCTION

The '*Really WILD Food Guide*' is written with outdoors people - and those who want to explore Britain's wild food resources - in mind. The project came about as the result of a personal interest in wild food plants and many conversations revolving round alternative medicine and wild food sources with a friend who is involved with outdoor activities in a big way. He is also a dab hand with a wok and no doubt terrifies anything that hops, leaps, swims in water or shimmies under stones. It was felt that so much knowledge about old and naturally wild foodstuffs has been totally forgotten by a population weaned on TV dinners, shrunk-wrapped meat and frozen veggies, and yet outdoors folk brush against potential wild ingredients for their next meal on a virtually daily basis.

In terms of modern-speak this guide is about 'empowering' readers to explore the world of wild food... a new landscape of tastes, textures and food experiences. The recipes cover a range of styles and try, where possible, to use ingredients that you would only expect to find naturally occurring in the wild. There are exceptions of course – particularly those goodies that outdoors people like to squirrel away in a rucksack for their cross-country travels... The odd onion, which makes such a difference to cooking, various sources of carbohydrate, assortments of dried spices, Kendal mint cake and whatever.

Readers trained in survival skills will recognize the emergency foods covered here, however the aim is really to encourage general use and exploration of wild foods - by folks camping outdoors and perhaps wanting to extend their food supplies, and for country folk curious enough to explore the possibilities of what the fields and hedgerows beyond their front door have to offer.

For these reasons some of the recipes may occasionally seem to fall between two stools. The camper may not be able to bake or casserole something, and the home cook is likely to have access to vastly more ingredients and cooking resources not available to anyone scuttling around the outdoors. However, it is all about the adaptability, and it is hoped readers will regard the recipes as starting points to adapt and explore as circumstances dictate. After all, if you were really reliant on wild food you would necessarily be opportunistic in using those food resources as they became available. On occasion you are certainly going to find that there is only a handful of ingredients available, requiring combination with secondary ingredients. That is where your increasing knowledge of wild plant foods will help you mix and match. Readers with a professional interest in living out of mess tins will hopefully find a few ways to brighten up tedious survival food.

If you are new to the world of wild foods you need to be aware that you will be pushing the envelope of your experiences with food and eating habits. Veteran outdoors people know from their experience of the elements that taking sensible precautions is a matter of course, and you need to adopt a similar mindset.

This is not about opening up a can of baked beans and chucking the contents down your throat... it is about getting to know wild foodstuffs and how you react to them. In a sense it is a journey of self-discovery.... the thing is not to be frightened of this unknown world but being sensibly cautious, and understanding that somewhere along the line you may well have a bad reaction to one of these unfamiliar foodstuffs. If that is a risk you find unacceptable, then stick to baked beans and TV dinners and throw away this guide. It is not for you.

IMPORTANT NOTE - READ

Three things are crucial to sourcing and eating wild food and need to be mentioned. First, it is imperative that you identify the plants mentioned here CORRECTLY. When out foraging for wild food always use a good botanical Field Guide, preferably two so you can cross-reference identification details. If you cannot identify something AVOID it. For example Angelica, Cow Parsley, Fools Parsley and Hemlock all belong to the same family and can look similar to the untrained eye - the latter two will kill you. So if you don't know what you are looking at never use it. Don't even consider 'pretty sure' as an option. Always be certain and safe, not dead.

Secondly, you need to test your tolerance to the plants mentioned here and be aware that your palate will need to adjust to the unfamiliar tastes and textures. Yes, hamburgers, monosodium glutamate and E-numbers the length of banknote serial numbers have a lot to answer for.

We are all so accustomed to pre-packed, tinned and standardised food that your body may need to adjust to the wild sort. As you will know, some people are allergic to certain foodstuffs – something as innocuous as peanuts can cause allergic reactions in some people - and this is no less the case with wild foods. Although many of the plants listed in this guide have been consumed by humans for centuries it is worth testing your own first time reaction to them before using *any* in quantity. The first time try a pinch of the plant cooked and raw - depending on the instructions - and wait several hours to check your body's reaction. This process is a less severe form of the usual routine used in survival training for the testing of toxins in would-be plant food - the so-called 'Universal Edibility Test'. It also provides you with your first opportunity to taste some of these unusual food resources. If you have any adverse reaction - other than to an unfamiliar taste - avoid the plant. To be perfectly honest the author finds the taste of some wild plants revolting - but then it's all down to a matter of taste, isn't it?

Incidentally, there are several very poisonous plants mentioned in this guide - Arum for example - which can be lethal unless treated correctly. If you are in the slightest bit unsure of dealing with these plants - DON'T! Leave them <u>well</u> alone! Should you decide to experiment with them be very cautious in your approach to testing.

Also, in the interest of safety wild fungi have not been included in the guide as it can be very difficult for untrained folks to identify fungi with certainty. If you happen to be a trained mycologist then you are going to have lots of fun bringing that knowledge to spice up and alter many of the recipes.

There are also a number of plants which can cause contra-indications in certain medical conditions. Where knowledge of this is known to the author these plants are marked with an asterisk '*' and you should always refer to the plant reference pages to check the potential contra-indication. If you have a **medical condition** it is important to do some extra background research to check how wild plants in the guide may affect you. 'Modern' medical herbals are one of the best ways to check this. If you do have a medical condition then wild foods are probably not a good choice for you. Sorry.

Lastly, there are the legal aspects of obtaining wild plants. There are quite a large number of endangered plants which are protected by the Wildlife & Countryside Act [WCA] 1981. The WCA forbids the intentional picking, uprooting or destruction of protected plants, and makes it illegal for any 'unauthorized' person to uproot *any* plant. Essentially, this means you have to have the permission of the landowner to dig up a plant. A growing plant is the property of the landowner and therefore subject to ordinary law.

At the time of writing none of the plants in this guide appear to be in the relevant WCA Schedule 8 but it is advisable to look at the DEFRA website to keep up to date on the changing legal status of UK wildlife and for more details on the legal aspects of wild plants.

In the general interest of conservation of plant stocks only 'harvest' where there is more than a sufficient supply to feed you – give those solitary specimens or small groups of plants time to propagate, then you can come back and get them another year. Of course, this doesn't apply to those abundant weeds which need a helping hand in their control.

One thought to leave you with. Foraging and preparing wild food takes time... In getting to know a particular landscape and what it can provide, collecting your ingredients, and then physically preparing them. Maybe supermarkets do have a purpose in life after all! But then maybe we are over reliant upon them.

Lastly, future editions of the guide may include a section of recipes from readers or these might be placed on the web pages. So if you have a wild food dish that you've conjured up and would like to share with others, and would like it to be considered for inclusion, drop the author an e-mail at the address below.

That's it. Have fun. Explore the unknown. And get *Really* **Wild** about your food.

JJ - December 2002

e-mail: wildfoodjj@yahoo.co.uk

WILD PLANT REFERENCE SECTION

Many of the plants that we now regard as 'wild' were once cultivated or used centuries ago for food but have since fallen into disuse. Some of those listed here were also regarded as 'famine foods' - fallbacks for when the crops failed.

Flowering, and fruiting, times of plants are indicated at the end of each entry in reversed out text. However, there will be regional differences and, if the current changes in our weather continue to be as unpredictable as they are, this will also affect flowering and fruiting times.

In itself the use of some of these historical plants provides us with a glimpse into the culinary and social world of our ancestors, while presenting many of us today with a whole new world of tastes and textures to explore. Perhaps the greatest difference, however, is that today we have a huge range of food technology available to call upon, and vastly more ingredients that can be bought off the supermarket shelf and which can enhance our use of these wild foodstuffs. Spices that were once worth their weight in gold we can now simply buy over the counter, while tomatoes, peppers and aubergines would all have been regarded as luxuries beyond the pocket of most, or quite simply unknown.

With the vast array of modern foodstuffs at our elbow the question is what can we do with those old wild ingredients? For those frequenting the outdoors on a regular basis the recipes in this guide are about inspiring them to recognize and be creative with the wild foods which are all around them. For 'foodies' it's more about providing ideas that encourage exploration of the tastes and textures - some of which you are bound to dislike - and inspire you to explore further.

What is not included within these reference pages are more common fruits which may have escaped into the wild, or lurked there for generations, and which really need no introduction - blackcurrants, blackberries, raspberries, gooseberries, plums, apples and so on.

If you are unfamiliar with *any* wild plant ingredient in a recipe it is important to refer back to this section to make sure you understand how the plant is used. Some are poisonous when raw, but fine when cooked. You will also find that many of the leaf greens respond to cooking like spinach, in that they seem to disappear to nothing in the pan.

A number of wild plants which are sometimes quoted as edible - bracken fiddleheads, comfrey and tansy - have not been included as there is research around which suggests that these plants may contain carcinogenic constituents. Of course, if you were in a survival situation such niceties would be set aside in favour of staying alive. Incidentally, if you have a medical condition do check the plants in this section before using them as some have contra-indications. Also, only ever use wild plant leaves which are fresh. Discard any dead, discoloured and dying ones as these can contain toxins.

One final thought to leave with you is one about conservation. Some wild plants are protected under the Wildlife & Countryside Act 1981, although none of these – as far as the author can determine - are included in the guide. However, there are some similar family members related to those mentioned which need to be preserved. That 'protection' is there for good reason so please play your part in preserving them, and for less common wild plants take only those which you need, leaving enough behind to ensure continued propagation of the stock or resource.

Incidentally, the plant reference section began life as a series of notes put together over several years by the author as an aide-memoire to the many wild plants which have edible parts, and has been developed further for the guide. It is hoped the reader will find it useful too.

KEY TO SYMBOLS

For a generalized and very *quick visual reference only* most entries in the Plant Reference Section have symbols identifying the parts usually regarded as edible. After that it is *most important* to read further to check on the preparation process for the identified plant parts.

❀ Flowers or flower parts

✿ Leaves, stems or shoots

🌶 Seeds or fruits

🌱 Roots or underground parts

Ʊ Contains edible sap

¹ ² ³ Annual, biennial or perennial

Alexanders - *Smyrnium olusatrum* ❀ ✿ ✿

The base stems, leaves and shoots are sort of celery-like in their appearance and in usage. The spring stems, stripped of their leaves can be boiled and used as a pot-herb. Stems may be simply blanched or cooked for about 10 minutes, the shoots cooked like asparagus, and the flower buds eaten raw. The aromatic black seeds can be used as a condiment. [2] **F 4-6 / FR 6-8**

Amaranth - *Amaranthus hypochondriacus* ✿ ✿

The dried seeds of amaranth, which reaches 5-6 feet in height, can be ground and made into a quite respectable pleasant, nutty-tasting low-gluten flour, and can be used for baking unlevened bread. The leaves were once used as a vegetable and in soups. The seeds can be 'sprouted' or cooked like rice until the water is just absorbed. Varieties of amaranth have been used across the world as a source of edible seed for centuries. In her book '*A Modern Herbal*' Mrs Grieve quotes the leaves of *A. blitum* being consumed in France like spinach.

Wild Angelica - *Angelica sylvestris* – WARNING ✿ ⚘

A. sylvestris is the wild version, and not the garden variety, of angelica. Do not confuse with water hemlock. The roots and stalks are the main useful parts and should be peeled before boiling, although the leaves are also edible boiled. Roots known to have been used as a source of flour for bread-making. [3] **F 7-9**

Contra-indication - large quantities may paralyze.

Garden Arrach / Mtn. Spinach - *Atriplex hortensis* ✿

If you are really stretched for edible greens then the leaves of this plant can be used as a spinach-like substitute.

Arrowhead - *Sagittaria latifolia* ⚘

Below ground this plant produces bulb-like, walnut-sized tubers which can grow up to a metre away from the main plant root system. The tubers, which are available all year round, are full of starch and have a potato-like taste and texture [perhaps the reason for one variety of the plant being nicknamed the Duck Potato], and should be boiled or roasted. They are best with the skin removed. At one time the dried roots were ground as a flour. [3] **F 5-7**

Ash - *Fraxinus excelsior* ✎

The 'keys' of this common tree can be made into an interesting pickle. Harvest them in the early autumn. **F 4-5**

Mtn. Ash / Rowan - *Sorbus aucuparia* ✎

A familiar tree with its clusters of red-orange berries in the autumn. The berries contain citric and malic acids [sources of vitamin C] and sugars, but are too bitter to eat raw and are usually stewed with sugar to produce rowan jelly. Generally the consensus seems to be that the berries are at their best once they have been touched by a couple of autumn frosts. In parts of Europe the dried berries were ground into flour and then used in the production of a spirit. **F 5-6**

Barberry - *Berberis vulgaris*

In the Middle Ages the barberry shrub was planted for both culinary purposes and ornamentation. It can be found in the wild but less so than once was the case. Mixed with sugar a jelly was made from the longish cylindrical deep red berries which are edible in the autumn and contain lots of vitamin C. Sauces made from the berries can accompany meat dishes, and in the Caucasus they are sometimes dried and ground as a seasoning. A few leaves may be added to salads and the fruits were also pickled. `F 5-6 / FR 9-10`

Beeches - *Fagus sylvatica*

Beech trees produce nuts - called masts - which are a good source of oil and protein, although the masts are fiddly to work with. In the author's experience the older nuts don't always contain a developed kernel, or have been got at by a grub which leaves a tell-tale hole in the shell. One way of generally guaranteeing something is to pick unopened pods and place these in a warm dry place which should see the plump masts fully exposed within a matter of hours.

Peeling the masts to get at the kernel is an unadventurous task for moments of downtime. Life is made easier if the masts are quickly fried for about a minute in a little hot oil, just till they brown [don't burn them], which makes the outer husk more brittle and easier to remove. This is a good method for the freshest masts which are fleshier and taste more hazelnut-like. Overheating reduces the size of the masts.

A second method tried by the author is to place the masts in an oil-free pan and heat as if making popcorn. After a couple of minutes the masts will begin to 'pop'. Remove the pan from the heat but occasionally lower over again until most of the masts have popped. Allow to cool and peel. Very fresh masts will sometimes explode their contents just like popcorn. Yet other methods include boiling the masts for 5 minutes in water to soften the outer husk, or baking in a cool oven for about 10-15 minutes to brittle the shells and aid hulling.

Although the kernels can be ground for stuffing, or to extract the tiny amount of oil they contain, they are really nicer as a source of a nutty texture and taste within dishes. Once you get the knack of shelling masts you should be able to accumulate about ½ cup of them in an hour. `F 4-5 / FR 9-10`

Bellflowers

Several members of this group with their large bell-shaped flowers but bitter, milky juice are edible, but the edible parts are specific to individual plants as follows: **Creeping Bellflower** [*Campanula rupunculoides*] the white-ish tubers of pre-flowering plants [also known as rampions] cooked. One old source said they are *'very good as a vegetable, to be used like radishes.'* With **Giant Bellflower** [*Campanula latifolia*] the young shoots are cooked like spinach. **Nettle-leaved Bellflower** [*Campanula trachelium*] young shoots are cooked like a green vegetable. [3] `F 6-9`

Birch - *Betula alba / pendula* ⊔

With its silvery papery bark the birch is a beautiful tree, and around March it produces large quantities of sap which are sometimes fermented to produce birch wine.

Bistort - *Polygonum bistorta* ✿ ⚲

The roots of the bistort contain lots of starch but have an astringent bitter taste which can be removed by soaking in water followed by roasting. The young shoots and leaves are also edible as a spring green, after boiling. [3] **F 5-7**

Bladder Campion - *Silene vulgaris* ✿

The young shoots of this plant have a pea-like taste but need to be boiled for ten minutes. [3] **F 5-9**

Borage - *Borago officinalis* ✾ ✿

Some observers would say that borage is not a wild plant at all, but more of a garden inhabitant. However, it has escaped in such quantities that it can commonly be found in the wild and is a useful edible plant. The flowers, and cucumber-ish flavoured young leaves, can be incorporated into salads, while older leaves and plant tops can be used as a pot-herb. Older leaves are a bit hairy and probably best not used in salads, but cooked instead. The flowers can be candied and older leaves dipped in batter and fried. A useful plant. [1] **F 5-9**

Brooklime - *Veronica beccabunga* – WARNING ✿

The fresh young leaves and shoots of the brooklime are slightly bitter but have a high vitamin content and can be used like watercress. The spring plant was once used in the fight against scurvy. However, the leaves should be eaten sparingly. [3] **F 5-8**

Broom - *Cytisus scoparius* – WARNING ✾

In old times the flower buds of our native broom were sometimes pickled. If you want to try this be absolutely certain that you are dealing with *Cytisus scoparius* and not Spanish Broom [found in gardens and as an escapee] or any other broom variety which may be poisonous. **F 5-6**

Contra-indication – don't use if suffering from hypertension and during pregnancy. Large quantities can cause paralysis.

Buckwheat - *Fagopyrum esculentum* ✿ ✎

The broadleaved buckwheat is not a member of the wheat family at all but a relation of the rhubarb family, and is therefore gluten free. Yet the size of the grain or nut - technically it is a fruit and is shaped a bit like a beech mast - makes it a potentially valuable food plant. Using buckwheat in the wild will depend on the reader's patience since the outer husk or hull must be removed and then the grit inside roasted in oil. In *'A Modern Herbal'* Mrs Grieve quoted the Japanese as using the young leaves as a vegetable. [1] **F 7-9**

Viper's Bugloss - *Echium vulgare* ✿

The leaves of this may be cooked like spinach. [3] `F 6-9`

Burdock - *Arctium lappa* ✿ ⚘

The leaves, stalks and roots of the burdock - which the Japanese cultivate for food - are edible subject to preparation. Overall the plant has a somewhat bitter taste which may or may not be to your liking but is easily removed by variously soaking in water or boiling. The spring leaves are prepared by boiling with two changes of water, while the thumb-width roots [high in fibre and up to 12 inches in length] of 'first year' plants need their outer skin peeling or scraping off, cutting or shredding into pieces and then boiling or soaking in one or two changes of water depending on your tolerance of the bitterness. Acidified water will stop the roots discolouring in the air. Generally the roots are more tender when cut very thin and steamed or simmered, and have a texture a little bit like bamboo shoots.

Young, pre-flowering leaf and flower stalks need to be peeled but may be eaten raw or cooked. As Gerard said, the stalks are best: '...*before the burres come forth, [with] the rinde pilled off, being eaten raw with salt and pepper, or boyled in the broth of fat meate, is pleasant to be eaten.*' As a biennial plant - producing growth and foliage the first year then flowering and expiring in year two - you will know whether a burdock plant is in its 'first year'. The peeled young stalks of the **lesser burdock** [*Arctium minus*] may be boiled and chopped for salads and broths. [2] `F 7-8`

Great Burnet - *Sanquisorba officinalis* ✿

Boil the tasty young leaves or eat them raw. [3] `F 6-9`

Salad Burnet - *Poterium sanguisorba* ✿

The salad burnet is an edible relic from yesteryear and was once cultivated for food. Older leaves can be tough and it was therefore the young spring and summer leaves with their cucumber-ish taste which made their way into salads, stews and soups. The secret of cultivation was to nip out the flower buds and flowers to promote growth of new young leaves. [3] `F 5-6`

Butcher's Broom - *Ruscus aculeatus* – WARNING ✿

Very much a plant of the south of England, the young shoots of the butcher's broom may be treated like those of asparagus. `F 1-4`

Contra-indication – don't use if you suffer from hypertension.

Caraway - *Carum carui* – WARNING ✿ ✐ ⚘

Caraway is one of the wider parsley family which includes poisonous Hemlock, so it is vital you identify the plant correctly before using.

Caraway seed is probably the product from this plant which is most familiar to people. However, salads may be enhanced by young spring leaves, which may also be added to soup, while older leaves may be boiled as a pot-herb vegetable. The roots may be boiled and used as a parsnip-like substitute. [2] F 4-7

Carrageen Moss - *Chondus crispus* ✿

A common, small bushy, purple-brown seaweed found around our coastline which can be washed and used in soups or stocks, boiled [3 parts liquid to 1 part seaweed] to produce a jelly, dried for future use [goes a pale beige-white colour], or even eaten raw. Best in May-August period when still young. Be careful where you gather this from as some parts of our coastlines are heavily polluted.

Catmint - *Nepata cataria* ✿

Catmint used to grow in the garden of the author's childhood home, but at the time it was never considered for any culinary purpose. However, in 'A Modern Herbal' Mrs Grieve alludes to the French harvesting the young shoots and leaves for seasoning. Interesting proposition, but still untried by the author so far. [3] F 7-9

Catsear - *Hypochoeris radicata* ✿

Use the young leaves in summer salads. [3] F 5-9

Wild Celery / Smallage – *Apium gravolens* ✿

Usually found in damp areas near coastlines this is the bitter fore-runner of our modern celery, and eaten by the ancient Romans. Leaves blanched by light exclusion are more tolerable. Much stronger tasting, add dried leaves to stocks and soups where modern celery might be used. [2] F 6-8

Charlock / Wild Mustard / Field Mustard - *Sinapsis arvensis* ✿🌾

The leaves, stems and seeds of charlock have various uses. The young leaves and buds are dealt with like spinach and provide a source of green vegetables in late winter and early spring; the stems, stripped of their peel and boiled, may be eaten at a push; the seeds are an alternative to mustard. [1] F 3-6

Chickweed - *Stellaria media* ✿

Chickweed has to be one of the most succulent and tender greens available to the outdoors person; growing as it does almost anywhere, and being available for most of the year. Young chickweed is tender enough to eat raw on its own - with a little dressing - or in salads or with scrambled eggs, while slightly older specimens can simply be wilted with a knob of butter in a pan and heated till cooked. Older specimens get a bit 'stalky' and you may want to remove the thicker stems before cooking. The tiny flowers are also edible. [1] F 3-10

Wild Chicory / Succory - *Chicorum intybus* – WARNING ✿ 🌿

Chicory can be a bit bitter for some people and in these instances it needs to be treated like the dandelion. The leaves can be used fresh in salads, or boiled like spinach, though if you don't like the bitter taste you may want a couple of changes of cooking water. The roots are also edible boiled, and are the source of chicory 'coffee' once dry roasted and ground. [3] F 7-9

A contra-indication with chicory is that it may cause problems with the retina if large amounts are consumed, or the plant is used on a continued basis.

Red Clover - *Trifolium pratense*

Red Clover is edible. The leaves can be eaten raw in salads but are better boiled. The red flowers can be added to salads, although one suggestion is to dip them in batter and then fry. The flowers can also be dried and added to soups and stews, or ground and small amounts added to baking flour. Eating clover leaves in excess can apparently cause bloating. [3] F 5-9

Common Cornsalad / Lamb's Lettuce - *Valerianella locusta*

An old staple food plant of yore the cornsalad or lamb's lettuce provides leaves for salads or a hot vegetable when cooked like spinach. Rich in vitamins and minerals, varieties of the plant are cultivated by the French for the table. Cornsalad appears from late winter onwards, with the best leaves growing in spring and autumn according to Mrs Grieve. [1] F 4-5

Corn Spurrey - *Spergula arvensis*

Corn spurrey is another of those plants which had a useful purpose in past times, being grown as both a fodder crop and as a source of food. For humans it was the seeds which were of importance, being mixed with other seeds and for meal, though the flowers don't smell pleasant. [1] F 6-10

Costmary / Alecost - *Chrysanthemum balsamita*

As the common name suggests this plant was once used in making beer – as a flavouring. A few young leaves can be used in salads and soups, as a poultry flavouring and, of course, in beer. Leaves can be dried. F 6-7

Couch Grass - *Agropyron repens*

The sweet-tasting roots of the couch grass were once used as a famine crop when the harvests failed, the dried roots being ground into flour for bread. In his book '*Wild Foods of Great Britain*' Cameron suggested the roots can be cooked like asparagus. [3] F 6-7

Cowslip - *Primula veris* – WARNING

Although technically not endangered or 'protected' the cowslip with its distinctive display of yellow flowers is under pressure from modern farming techniques, so only take a *few* leaves to try if there are a sufficient number of plants to harvest from. The leaves were once incorporated into salads and also combined with other herbs in meat stuffing. [3] F 4-5

Contra-indication – don't use cowslip if you suffer from allergies.

Cuckoopint / Lords & Ladies ☠ - *Arum maculatum* – WARNING

The cuckoopint or lord and ladies comes with a **severe hazard warning**. The entire plant is poisonous and the berries can be fatal if consumed. However, the acrid tasting roots, which are about the size of a pigeon egg, may be eaten once they have been well roasted. As yet the author has been unable to obtain a supply of cuckoopint to experiment with, so perhaps best avoid.

The roots also produce an arrowroot starch substitute [Portland Arrowroot and Portland Sago] which was obtained by boiling then drying and powdering the root. Again, the process of heat treatment and the drying de-nature the main toxic constituent of the plant. If you are unsure about handling and cooking arum, **do not use**. [3] **F 4-5**

Common Daisy - *Bellis perennis* ❀

Most sources on wild foods mention nothing about the common daisy though Mrs Grieve says that the acrid leaves are used in some countries as a pot-herb. With so many other wild vegetable plants around this is one the author has not yet succumbed to. [3] **F 3-10**

Common Dandelion - *Taraxacum officinale* – WARNING ❀ ❀ ☙

There are great claims for the culinary capabilities of the common dandelion but as far as this author is concerned the bitterness of the uncooked green leaves makes the toes curl. On the other hand, newly opening flowers are sweetish.

Young leaves are recommended for salads but they are still bitter, while older leaves are even more so. Dandelion is definitely an acquired taste. The leaves become more acceptable if they are given a couple of 5 minute boilings in two changes of water - use only the top two thirds of the leaf, discarding most of the stem part. The roots are used in Japanese cuisine, cooked, although they may be eaten raw in salads - something this author has not yet felt the urge to do given the bitterness of the leaves. In the past the roots were boiled then roasted and ground into a coffee substitute. Leaves can be blanched and frozen for later use.

If you have a static base then you might have time to 'earth-up' some dandelion plants to bleach them to an almost white state. This reduces the bitterness. Another alternative is to cover a plant with an upturned plant pot to achieve the same effect.

Despite the niggles, the dandelion is full of calcium, iron, beta-carotene, and vitamins A, B and C - 25 times more vitamin A than tomato juice. However, if you are double boiling your dandelion leaves a lot of goodness will go. [3] **F 3-9**

Contra-indication - Dandelion is diuretic in quantity. Not without reason was it called 'pisenlits' in the past.

Broad / Common Dock - *Rumex obtusifolius*
Although most parts of the plant are edible a couple of boilings are needed to take away some of the bitterness, though the roots need to be scraped. [3] F6-8
The Shore Dock, Rumex rupestris, is protected.

Curled / Sour / Yellow Dock - *Rumex crispus* – WARNING
Select young plants and use the youngest and tenderest leaves and boil - changing the water twice to remove the bitterness. [3] F 5-7

Contra-indications - in some individuals the raw sap may cause dermatitis, and excessive amounts of dock can cause nausea.

Dulse - *Palmaria palmata*
Found virtually everywhere around our coasts this red seaweed can be boiled like a vegetable after first washing and soaking in water. It can also be pan-fried, dry roasted, steamed and even eaten raw in salad. There is also the small **pepper dulse** [*Laurencia pinnatifida*] which only grows a few inches high. As the name suggests the fronds taste peppery.

Elcampane - *Inula helenium*
Roots once candied as a sweet, and also used to flavour sweets. [3] F 7-8

Elder - *Sambucus nigra*
The elder should need no introduction given its prodigious presence in the countryside. However, it is a shrub with a mixed reputation as a wild food. Only the frothy flower heads and the berries can be eaten, and in the case of the latter some writers find the taste unpleasant. This author has not found that to be the case, choosing only the ripest of the little black berries which, in fact, have very little taste but do have a bothersome raspberry-like seed. One suggestion to concentrate the flavour of the berries is to dry them - spread out and dried in the sun, or put on an oven tray and placed in a very low heat till dry. The flower buds can be pickled. The sprays of flowers can be added to summer drinks or dipped in batter, fried and then dusted with sugar. F 6-7

Evening Primrose - *Oenothera biennis*
Once grown on the continent as a food the young leaves are edible cooked or raw, while the roots may be eaten raw, cooked or pickled. Slightly sweet tasting roots best gathered in autumn and winter. [2] F 6-9

Fat-Hen / Goosefoot - *Chenopodium album*
Another of the staple foods of our forebears - with a variety of sub-species - lamb's quarters as this wild plant is sometimes known, has to be one of the most nutritious plants of the hedgerow and fields with high concentrations of minerals and vitamin B1.

The leaves, which have a spinach-ish taste, are generally cooked in the same way as spinach, but may also be eaten raw. In times past it was common for the dried seeds to be ground into a black flour. [1] F 7-10

Fennel - *Foeniculum vulgare* – WARNING ✿ ⚲
The bulb-like root of fennel and the stalks have been used as a vegetable, and the leaves as salad and soup ingredients through history. Can be boiled, dried off and dipped in flour before being fried. [3] F 7-10

Contra-indications - consumption of large quantities can upset the nervous system.

Flowering-rush - *Butomus umbellatus* ⚲
In Russia the roots are apparently eaten. [3] F 7-8

Goat's Rue / French Lilac - *Galega officinalis* – WARNING ✿
Make sure you do not confuse this plant with any of the vetch family which look similar but can be poisonous. Juice from the plant can be used to clot milk in cheese-making. Gerard said: *'The herbe itselfe is eaten, being boiled with flesh, as we use to eate Cabbage.... and likewise in sallades, with oile, vineger and pepper...'* Modern sources caution usage of this quite powerful plant. [3] F 6-7

Good King Henry - *Chenopodium bonus-henricus* ✿
Growing up to about 2 feet high the young leaves of GKH have long been used as a spinach-like vegetable which crops almost all year round. While useful as a pot-herb and in broth, the young leaves and shoots are also edible raw, although the shoots - which can be cooked like asparagus - really need to be peeled to make them less stringy. If you find the taste a little bitter boil in two changes of water. [3] F 4-10 Chamberlin reported that the Gosiute indians also collected and extensively used the seeds of the **strawberry-blite** [*C. capitatum* [1] F 7-8], and **red goosefoot** [*C. rubens* [1] F 5-9] both of which can be found in the UK. Zuni indians mixed similar ground grains with corn meal which was made into a stiff batter subsequently formed into balls or patties for steaming.

Goosegrass / Cleavers - *Galium aparine* ✿ ✎
Cleavers are a menace to farmers, their invasive clinging stems choking hedgerows and unattended corners of fields. Mrs Grieve mentions that the young shoots were once boiled, although other writers recommend that the plant is better steamed than boiled [it is not particularly palatable but it is high in vitamin C]. The plant is also best used before the seeds form; these, in turn, were once dried then roasted and used as a coffee substitute. The dried plant can also be used as a tea. Large amounts of goosegrass can be laxative. [1] F 6-9

Ground-elder / Goutweed - *Aegopodium podagraria* ✿
Once upon a time this plant was thought by herbalists to be a cure for gout, hence the name. However, the strong flavoured [disagreeable to many] young

leaves can be boiled like spinach or in salty water as a vegetable and pot-herb. The young leaves may also be used in salads. [3] F 5-8

Ground Ivy / Ale-hoof - *Nepeta glechoma* ✿

Young leaves may be eaten, but are bitter. Leaves dried and used as a tea. One old reference mentions a conserve being made of the leaves in spring. [3] F 7-9

Guelder Rose ☠ - *Viburnum opulus* - WARNING 🍃

The fruits of the guelder, also known as the cranberry tree, are regarded as rather a second class substitute for cranberries. If you do decide to use them then the berries MUST be cooked before eating as they are poisonous raw. F 5-7

Hairy Bittercress - *Cardamine hirsuta* ✿ 🍃

The hairy bittercress is a less peppery and spicy alternative to the cuckooflower or lady's smock and can be used in salads or as a vegetable. Try adding to sandwiches to provide a little lift. The whole plant is edible. [1] F 5-6

Hawthorn - *Crataegus* ✿ ✿ 🍃

There are many varieties of the hawthorn in the UK and it is the experience of the author to encounter berries - which are edible raw or cooked - that were not particularly tasty. There is a certain sweetness to the creamy pulp, but there is also an after-taste that the author does not like. The other problem is that the haws are mainly all seed, though there are reportedly much more fleshy varieties. Boiled and sieved the pulp could be used in thickening soups or stews, while a haw jelly is sometimes made. In the author's opinion a much better alternative is to use the budding leaves and spring leaf growth raw in salads. Try the buds in a traditional mayonnaise potato salad. F 5-6

Hawkbits / Hawkweeds ✿

These plants are part of the extended daisy family and in '*Honey from a Weed*' by Patience Gray there is mention that in Mediterranean countries it is common for them to be collected for salads. In the UK the leaves of the **rough hawkbit** [*Leontodon hispidus*] can be used as a summer salad vegetable. [3] F6-9 *Hierarcium attenuatifolium, zetlandicum,* and *northroense* are all protected.

Hazelnut - *Corylus avellana* 🍃

The hazel needs no introduction, though its cultivated cousin the 'cobnut' may do. Ripening in the autumn hazelnuts may also be eaten in their unripe state; and can provide extra texture to a cooked dish where the addition of a nutty texture is sought. F 1-3 / FR 9-10

Herb Bennett / Wood Avens - *Geum urbanum* ✿ ⚘

The old common name for this plant was 'clove root' because of its mild spicy rhizome which was dried for use, and was employed in medieval times as a pot-herb in soups. Add young leaves to salads. [3] F 6-8

Hogweed/Cow Parsnip - *Heracleum sphondylium* – WARNING ✿ ⚕

This is another of the extended parsley family and as such needs to be identified with great care, it should also not be confused with the **giant hogweed** [*Heracleum mantegazzianum*]. The roots may be eaten but they are not very palatable. A better bet are the cooked young shoots early in the summer and the peeled stalks. [2] [3] F 5-10

Contra-indication - the sap from the plant can cause blistering of sensitive skin, particularly in the presence of sunlight. Can also cause permanent pigmentation change.

Hop - *Humulus lupulus* ✿

Well known for its inclusion in beer the straggly tendrils of the hop can be found in many hedgerows. The stem fibres have been used for making cloth while the young shoots, leaves and foliage are edible. The young shoot tips and male flowers can be used in salad or blanched and used as a pot-herb, and young foliage of the late spring and early summer cooked like asparagus. [3] F 5-8

Horseradishes - *Armoracia* – WARNING ✿ ⚕

Preparing horseradish sauce from the grated root of this plant has made many a cook cry, such is the strength of it. Both the roots and the spring leaves may be eaten raw, or boiled in salted water. F5-6

Contra-indication - large quantities will inflame the gut.

House-leek - *Sempervivum tectorum* ✿

Growing on rooftops and walls the spiky young leaves and shoots of the plant can be eaten. Gerard says it is: '...*used in many places in sallads, in which it hath a fine relish, and a pleasant taste...*' Eaten in Eastern Europe. [3] F 6-7

Japanese Knotweed - *Polygonum cuspidatum* ✿

Found in gardens, on urban wasteland and town fringes - and therefore not truly 'wild' - knotweed is regarded as a very troublesome plant. However, the young spring shoots may be cooked like asparagus. Peel older stalks and use like rhubarb in jams and pies - it has a lemony flavour. In that respect it can sort of provide a rudimentary replacement to lemongrass in Thai-type curries. The plant is regarded as a serious pest and it is illegal to introduce knotweed into the wild. [3] F 8-10

Jerusalem Artichoke - *Helianthus tuberosus* ⚕

A cultivated plant that you will sometimes find as escapees in the wild. This is a type of sunflower and is unrelated to the artichoke proper, having yellow flowers and good tasting irregular tubers - up to about 4-5 inches long and 2 inches wide - that taste of artichoke. The tubers are at their best towards the end of the year. Unlike many other wild tubers mentioned in this guide they contain little starch. They are, however, very versatile and can be baked, boiled, sliced and fried, pickled, or even eaten raw. The raw tuber discolours in the air once it has been peeled and should be dipped into acidulated water to stop this - if eating raw serve with lemon juice to prevent same.

Juniper - *Juniperus communis* - WARNING 🌿

The spicy and aromatic berries of juniper are far too astringent to be eaten on their own as a fruit. Added to meat dishes - particularly game - they come into their own, imparting a wonderful flavour. The berries can be used raw, or dried [sometimes roasted] and then used whole or crushed. **F 4-6 / FR 2-3**

Contra-indication – don't use if you have kidney problems or during pregnancy.

Kelp ✤

There are several members of the kelp family which humans can consume - **oarweed** [*Laminaria digitata*], **dabberlocks** [*Alaria esculenta*] and **sugar kelp** [*Laminaria saccharina*] - which are variously found round our coastlines. Oarweed has a salty strong taste while sugar kelp has a sweetish taste as its name suggests.

Wash then tenderize kelp by soaking in water for an hour, or marinate. It can be simmered for about 15 minutes, pan-fried till crisp, or roasted in a moderately cool oven for about 5 minutes.

Lady's Smock / Cuckooflower - *Cardamine pratensis* ✿ ✤

Also known as bittercress it is odd to think that this rather unassuming looking herb plant - with its small lilac flowers - was once cultivated for use in salads and as a vegetable. The flowers and upper and young leaves can be used raw in salads, providing a peppery hint. Older leaves are much more so. The leaves can also be added to soups and cooked as a vegetable. [3] **F 4-6**

Laver - *Porphyra umbilicalis* ✤

Growing to about 6-8 inches long the purple laver turns black when exposed to air. However, with long boiling it can be transformed into a blackish-green gelatinous mass which can be used in cooking.

Lime - *Tilia x europaea* ✿ ✤ ⛝

The lime tree is common throughout the UK and provides refreshment in all sorts of ways. The dried young flowers [and only the young ones] can be infused to provide a tea and the unopened leaf buds and young leaves are edible raw. The leaves are quite glutinous when young and were often placed in sandwiches. Lime sap in spring contains much sugar. **F 7 / FR 7-10**

Lovage - *Levisticium officinale* – WARNING ✤ 🌿 ⚕

This is a garden plant which escapes into the wild and one that you need to treat with respect - see contra-indications below. Only **use in small quantities** until you know your tolerance to the plant. In the old days the dried root used to be powdered and used as a pepper substitute. The stem and leaf stalks can be blanched and used like celery; the leaves in soups, casseroles and sauces or as a vegetable; the dried seeds with meat; and the peeled roots boiled like a vegetable. Dry the leaves and use like a spice. The Scottish variety *Ligusticum scoticum* [3] F 6-8, also known as **sea lovage**, was once eaten as a vegetable in the quest to prevent scurvy.

Contra-indications - lovage should not be used in large quantities [the author recently read a report on the internet that stated 2 cups of chopped lovage had caused a group of diners to feel nauseous. The plant should also be avoided by anyone suffering with kidney disease.

Lucerne / Alfalfa - *Medicago sativa* ✿

The sprouted seed of alfalfa is well known to the health conscious, but if you happen to find the fully grown plant in the grass verges the leaves, which are high in vitamin A and D, may be used in salads or cooked as a vegetable. [3] F 6-7

Common Mallow - *Malva sylvestris* – WARNING ✿ 🌿 ᵞ

This is quite a common wild plant but is also grown in gardens from whence it escapes, and many of the mallow family have been used as food at some time. The basic quality of the common mallow is that its leaves produce a glutinous substance when cooked, and this is a perfect base for making soups. Indeed, in Egypt a sort of gloopy soup made of mallow is a common dish.

The leaves are available for a large part of the year right into winter. However, it is important to ensure that no brown leaf parts end up in any soup or stew you are making, or when cooking the leaves as a vegetable. The seeds can be snacked on or added to summer salads to add texture and flavour. [3] F 6-11

Contra-indications - large amounts can cause indigestion and be purgative.

Marsh Mallow - *Althaea officinalis* ᵞ

The fibrous white rootstock - surrounded by a yellow peel - contains starch and mucilage and can be boiled and then stir-fried. The mucilaginous nature of the rootstock means that water used in boiling the roots can be considered as a possible replacement for the albumen of egg whites in certain recipes. The tops and tender spring leaves have sometimes been used in salads. Culpepper describes the roots as providing: *'slimy juyce which being layd in water will thicken it as if it were gelly.'* The flower buds have been pickled. [3] F 7-9 *Rough Marsh Mallow, Althaea hirsuta, is protected.*

Manna Grass - *Glyceria aquatica & distans* 🌿

The seeds of the **reed manna** [*G. aquatica* [3] F 4-8] and **reflexed** [*G. distans*] [3] F 6-10 manna grasses were used as food by American indians.

Marsh Marigold - *Caltha palustris* – WARNING
Any use of the marsh marigold comes with a warning. Only three reference sources the author has found mention the plant's edibility - Mrs. Grieve in 'A Modern Herbal', US Army Field Manual FM21-76, and a report about the Menomini indians. These quote the leaves as edible if cooked like spinach. Other sources quote the plant as being poisonous but this is because of the toxin helleborin which is contained in the leaves and will be removed by a good boiling. However, the author has not yet had any chance to access a source of marsh marigolds to try out. Should you decide to try the plant do so with the greatest of caution and regard the plant as poisonous when raw and discard any liquor resulting from cooking - give any cooked leaves a final rinse in hot water for safety. [3] F 3-5

Marsh Woundwort - *Stachys palustris*
Chamberlin says the Gosiute gathered the seeds of this as food and ate the tuberous roots after being boiled. Young shoots cooked like asparagus. [3] F 7-9

Meadowsweet - *Filipendula ulmaria*
The pleasant tasting flowers are sometimes added to summer drinks or an infusion of same made as a herbal tea. [3] F 6-8

Common Melilot - *Melilotus officinalis* – WARNING
Also called yellow sweet clover, the dried herb and seeds have intense fragrancy and can be used in flavouring meat dishes like rabbit. The plant should only be used sparingly for flavouring, not for consumption. [2] F 5-9

Contra-indication - large amounts of the plant are emetic; however you should not be cooking this one as a vegetable anyway.

Mints - *Mentha* - WARNING
The problem with the mint family is that there are many of them and they frequently cross. **Peppermint** [*Mentha piperita* [3] F 8-10] is the result of a cross between the **water mint** [*Mentha aquatica* [3] F 7-10] and **spearmint** [*Mentha spicata* [3] F 8-9], while cultivated varieties frequently escape and are found in the wild. However, they have their uses. Peppermint and water mint are used as pot-herbs, and spearmint is generally used for mint sauce. The most commonly cultivated culinary varieties are the round-leaved and apple-scented mints.

Contra-indication – water mint can be emetic in large quantities and oil of peppermint can produce an allergic reaction.

Mugwort - *Artemisia vulgaris* - WARNING
A plant with a long history in medicine but also used in the past to flavour beer. It is used in Japan to flavour food. Particularly good with fatty meats and game birds. Use only occasionally and sparingly as mugwort can cause problems to the nervous system. [3] F 7-9

Black Mustard - *Synapsis nigra* - WARNING ✿ 🌿

Long cultivated for its seeds which are turned into the black mustard condiment [dry the mature seeds in the sun or warm air]. Apparently the Romans cooked the leaves as a vegetable, while the young leaves may be put into salads - they are high in vitamins A, B1 and 2 and C. The dried seeds can also be added to salads. Steam the broccoli-like buds for a few minutes while the leaves are treated like turnip greens or spinach for cooking purposes. Older leaves are more bitter and may require two changes of cooking water. [1] **F 6-9 / FR 7-9**

Contra-indication – can cause skin blistering when handled.

Garlic Mustard / Jack-by-the-Hedge - *Alliaria petiolata* ✿

Crushing the leaves of this plant [also known as Hedge Garlic] gives away its potential use - as a milder onion-like alternative to garlic proper. The pre-flowering upper leaves and shoots are the best, and may be boiled or used in sauces, while small quantities can be chopped and incorporated into salads. Later in the year the leaves get bitter but there is sometimes a second crop of shoots in the autumn. [2] **F 4-6**

Common Hedge Mustard - *Sisymbrium officinale* – WARNING ✿

Not as pungent as real mustard the plant was once used in soups and salads, and in sauces to accompany salt fish. Rather dust retentive. [1] **F 5-9**

Contra-indications - should not be consumed by anyone with a heart problem, or by very young children or the elderly.

White Mustard - *Synapsis alba* ✿

This is the cultivated form of mustard which ends up as the condiment. However, it ends up as a wild escapee too, and young seedlings and peppery leaves can be used raw in salads, and the whole plant can be cooked. [1] **F 6-9**   .

Common Nettle - *Urtica dioica* – WARNING ✿

Another plant which needs no introduction - unless you have never been stung by a nettle. Rich in vitamins C and A the plant is best used when it and the leaves are young. When only a few inches high the stalks and leaves are tender enough to be used entirely [and are virtually sting-free], however once the plant gets beyond about six inches tall the leaves remain the best part to be harvested [using gloves, of course]. As the plant gets older the texture becomes gritty and the leaves hairy. Once the plant begins to flower it is really beyond its useful stage - unless you are desperate. Where mature nettles have been cut down they will later develop new secondary young growth which may also eaten.

There are various ways of cooking the leaves or young plant - straight boiling in water for about 5-6 minutes, or blanching in boiling water for a couple of minutes and then sweating in a pan with some butter until tender. It is very much like cooking spinach, and the same goes for the shrinkage in volume.

The leaves can be dried and stored - hang whole stems then remove the leaves, or spread leaves out on a flat surface to dry in the sun. The expressed juice of the nettle can be used as a rennet substitute for making cheese. [3] F 6-10

Contra-indication - one source the author came across indicated that there was research showing that nettles may reduce blood-sugar and blood pressure.

Dead Nettles - *Lamium album* and *purpereum*

Cooked as a spinach-like vegetable [sweated with a knob of butter in a pan] or added to soups, the leaves and shoots of both red and white dead nettles are edible. One old reference mentions the flowers of *L. album* being made into a conserve – 1lb of flowers to 2lb of sugar. **Red dead nettle** [*L. purpereum*] was a useful winter pot-herb, while **hen-bit dead nettle** [*L. amplexicaule*] can also be eaten. *L. album* [3] F 4-10 / *L. purpuream & amplexicaule* [1] F 3-5

Nipplewort - *Lapsana communis*

The young leaves have a radishy flavour and can be used in salads or cooked like spinach as a green vegetable. [1] F 6-8

English Oak - *Quercus robur*

Many readers will be familiar with the image of pigs troughing on windfall acorns, but what is less well known is that they offer humans with a food source too [protein, carbohydrate and Calcium] providing the acorns are prepared properly.

The basic problem with raw acorns is that **they contain huge amounts of tannin which will make you extremely ill if not removed**, and this is achieved by leaching out the tannin with water. The American indians used to leave shelled acorns in streams for weeks, but this is not a practical proposition if you are in the outdoors or have metered water. Be aware, too, that the process takes lots of water. In '*Useful Wild Plants*' Saunders talked of the indians pounding acorns [not the same varieties as the English oak, mind], then layering these on a sieve structure and pouring warm water over for several hours.

There seem to be various contemporary methods touted round for the leaching process, though there is more agreement on the fact that the chosen acorns should be bug and disease-free, and that windfall or brown-to-tanned acorns should be used rather than green ones picked from the tree. Begin by removing the shell - the easiest method being to slit the acorn skins, place in a bowl and pour boiling water and leave for a while or, alternatively, slit and then boil for 5 minutes. The slit will widen and the shells become more pliable.

On the cooking side... The American army favours boiling shelled acorns for a couple of hours then soaking in cold water for 3-4 days changing the water occasionally; after which the acorns are ground and cooked up. Another method proffered suggests boiling in several changes of water each boiling lasting an hour. Yet another method suggests that the shelled acorns are crushed [provides more surface area for the water to work on] and then steeped and boiled. If you have a blender available the latter is a quick way of producing a chunky acorn mash; the colour of the mixture reminiscent of times when making hummus. When following this method of preparation the author vigorously boils the ground acorns for ten minutes then changes the water - replacing the evil-looking brown-black liquor with fresh boiling water - and repeats the process every 10-15 minutes for about an hour, followed by several final soakings in hot water. Make sure to stir during the first 5-10 minutes of boiling to prevent the mash sticking to the bottom of the pan.

In any case, the boiling water will eventually run clear, and if you taste a bit of the acorn meat it will no longer be bitter, indicating that most of the tannin has been removed. What you end up with is a mush that has a sort of chocolate colour. This contains quite a lot of water and the excess can simply be removed by squeezing handfuls to express the water.

Depending on which route you have gone - keeping the acorns whole or crushed - the resulting acorns can be deep-fried, dried and ground as a flour addition, added to soups or used as a thickener, or dried in a slow oven and the brittle nuts used as a trail food.

The acorns of other oaks are edible up to a point but some of them contain even more tannin than the English variety, so best stay with our native tree. If water is scarce or at a premium you may wish to ignore acorns as a food source. Boiled, leached acorns or the mash can be frozen. **F 4-5 / FR 9-10**

Ox-eye Daisy - *Chrysanthemum leucanthemum* ✿
The lighter young green leaves of the ox-eye are edible and Mrs Grieve mentioned that the Italians eat them in salads. [3] **F 6-7**

Bristly Ox-Tongue - *Helminthia echioides* ✿
A rather bitter plant which was once boiled and used as a pot-herb when in its young state. Also once used for making pickle. [1,2] **F 6-10**

Oysterplant - *Mertensia maritima* ✿
Increasingly less common, the leaves of the shore loving oysterplant can be eaten raw or cooked. [3] **F 6-8**

Cow Parsley / Wild Chervil - *Anthriscus sylvestris* – WARNING ✿
Another warning here as the cow parsley belongs to the same family as the poisonous hemlock and fool's parsley group. Avoid unless you are absolutely 100% certain of identification. The young leaves and stems can be used in stews and soups, but as the plant ages it becomes bitter. However, cow parsley can produce a second crop of leaves later in the year. The leaves may also be dried. [1] **F 4-8**

Parsley Piert - *Aphanes arvensis* ✿

Unrelated to the parsley family - tasting rather astringent - and, according to Mrs Grieve, Culpepper indicated that In the 17th century parsley piert was added to salads, used as a winter pickle, and even dried. [1] `F 4-10`

Field Pennycress - *Thlaspi arvense* ✿

This is one plant you may prefer to avoid as the bruised plant smells unpleasant, however the chopped leaves have been used in salads, and may be boiled or used in cooked dishes. Ground seeds a mustard substitute. It is a bothersome farm weed. [1] `F 4-6` *Perfoliate pennycress, Thlapsi perfoliatum, is protected.*

Pig Nut - *Conopodium majus* ☘

Pignuts were once regarded as a famine food, the edible, nutty flavoured, starch-rich round tubers being about six inches below ground. Young country children would dig the roots up and eat them raw. Roots can be added to stews, boiled or roasted like potatoes, but are not overly palatable. [3] `F 5-6`

Pine - *pinus species* ✿

The seeds of all the pines are edible. Just wait till the cones open and then roast seeds or eat them raw. The young green spring cones may also be boiled or baked. The leaves or 'needles' of pine are full of vitamin C and a healthy 'pine needle tea' can be made by infusing needles in hot water for 10-15 minutes.

Plantains - *Plantago* ✿

Plantains come in a variety of shapes and as far as the author is concerned they are more of a survival plant than something you would eat out of choice.

The young leaves of these may be used in stews, boiled like spinach, used as a pot-herb, and even eaten raw if one is to be believed. If you pick larger or older leaves then boiling in a couple of changes of water is the only route to removing the bitter taste.

In the **greater plantain** [*Plantago major*] only use the top 3 inches or so of older leaves, discarding the last inch or so of stem. By this stage in leaf development the veins are rather stringy. **Ribwort plantain** [*Plantago lanceolata*] is much less palatable. Even after two 5 minute boilings the 'ribs' seem to retain some bitter taste. And whoever suggested the leaves can be eaten raw must have been desperate. *P. major* [3] `F 5-11` / *P. lanceolata* [3] `F 6-10`

Common Red Poppy - *Papaver rhoeas* ✿

The young foliage of the common poppy can be used in salads but also used as a spinach-like vegetable. [1] `F 5-7`

Primroses - *Primula vulgaris* – WARNING ✿ ✿

If you are going to try primrose leaves make sure there is a large stock of the plant which you can select from. In some parts of the countryside primroses are in short supply, having being collected to virtual destruction. Do your bit to preserve those hard-hit stocks. All parts of the plant are edible and the leaves were once boiled as a vegetable green. Young leaves are good in salads. [3] F 2-5

Contra-indications - primroses may cause allergic reactions.

Common / Wild Purslane - *Portulaca oleracea*
The Victorians cultivated purslane as a pot-herb but you will sometimes find escapees in the wild. Most parts are edible - young pre-flowering shoots for salads, or boiled as a vegetable, or purslane seeds as a flour substitute or even eaten raw. The purslane is a good stew additive as it is slightly mucilaginous, and the dried seeds can be ground and used as a flour addition.

Mrs Grieve also mentions the **golden purslane** [*P. sativa*] and its cooling young shoots for salads. She even says that when a plant has run to seed the stems can be pickled in salt and vinegar.

Wild Radish - *Raphanus raphanistrum*
A common weed, the leaves and roots of which are edible. [1] F 5-9

Ramsons - *Allium ursinum*
Ramsons are the wild form of garlic and have a pungent smell when bruised. All parts of the plant can be used to flavour food, though it is unlike the usual culinary quality garlic you might expect to find at the supermarket. However, if you are out on the trail at least there is the option of adding the taste of garlic although cooking really diminishes that quality. If you want to use the very small bulb parts then be prepared to dig down at least 6 inches. [3] F 5

Field garlic [*A. oleraceum* [3] F 7-8] and **wild onion** [*A. vineale* [3] F 6-7] also have similar properties. Neither are really anything to shout about, the wild onion only producing small bulbs. However, both have been used as meat flavouring pot-herbs.

Rape - *Brassica napus* – WARNING
This is definitely not a wild flower and certainly not in short supply judging by the thousands of acres of land turned over to the cultivation of rape. The young pre-flowering spring leaves can be used in salads and the more tender tops and side shoots also used as spring greens. F 5-8

Contra-indication - the pollen of the rape may cause allergic reaction in people pre-disposed to hay-fever/asthma.

Common Reed - *Phragmites communis*
The common reed has an edible root similar to the bullrush mentioned below, and is peeled and boiled like potatoes. However, there is such little starch content compared to the bullrush, that you may decide to give this one a miss unless desperate for food. If the stems of growing plants are slit or punctured they exude an edible sugar-rich gum. [3] F 7-9

Reedmace/Cat's-tail - *Typha latifolia* [Greater] / *angustifolia* [Lesser]

These are the plants with cigar-like brown seed heads that we generally call bullrushes, and they are a potential goldmine of edible parts. The fibrous and starchy rootstocks are edible raw, boiled, or roasted and contain a small amount of sugar. Best collected in winter and early spring.

In some countries the white portions of pre-flowering shoots are eaten as a vegetable, being prepared like asparagus - they may also be pickled or stir-fried. The shoots, which contain potassium, vitamin C, niacin and riboflavin among other things, are covered by a sheath of outer leaves which needs to be peeled back to get at the shoot.

The young leaves may be cooked like spinach. The yellow pollen may be collected in quite large quantities by placing a bag over the heads of several plants and shaking off the pollen. This is then incorporated with flour to make bread, biscuits or pancakes, or can be mixed with water and steamed into a sort of bread. If using the roots for flour production then they are best collected during the winter, and then can be dried, ground and sifted, or pulverized in water and the sugary starch removed and dried in the air. This flour can be used as a corn starch replacement in some instances. [3] F 6-8

Common Rest-Harrow / Wild Liquorice - *Ononis repens*

As the common name suggests rest-harrow is associated with the taste of liquorice. Mrs Grieve identifies the young shoots of **goat's rest-harrow** [*Ononis arvensis*] as having been used boiled, in salads or pickled. However, the author has not as yet been able to verify this from other sources. [3] F 6-9 *Small Rest-Harrow, Ononis oreclinata, is protected.*

Rocket-salad - *Eruca vesicaria*

Add small amounts of the leaves to salad mixtures.

Rose Bay Willowherb - *Chamaenerion angustifolium* - WARNING

Such a bothersome weed! That is generally how the rose bay willowherb is regarded; particularly by gardeners who dread the fallout from clouds of air borne seeds drifting across their garden.

The young spring leaves, shoots, flowers and stems are said to be edible raw, however ***the leaves can have a stupifying effect*** and it is suggested that they are blanched or lightly boiled. By mid- to late summer the leaves have become tough. As the plant matures the pith in the stems becomes sweet-ish, and was once used for making ale and can be added to soups. The **broad-leaved willowherb** [*Epilobium montanum*] is also similarly said to be edible. [3] F 6-9

Wild Salsify / Vegetable Oyster - *Tragopogon porrifolius*

The purple flowered Tragopogon porrifolius is a type of goat's beard, and is unrelated to the oysterplant [*Mertensia maritima*]. The roots have the vaguest taste of seafood, hence the common name of vegetable oyster. Peel the white tapering taproots and boil. They have a habit of becoming discoloured; a situation remedied by putting the peeled roots into some acidulated water. The young leaves are edible boiled but should be used sparingly in salads.

Common Scurvygrass - *Cochlearia officinalis* ❀

A member of the cabbage family the common scurvygrass is a common plant of the coastline. The plant's main claim to fame is that it contains large amounts of vitamin C and, in the days when diets were bad and vitamins from citrus fruits were unavailable, people would drink a glass of scurvygrass water. Scurvygrass does not have a very pleasant smell and has a warm, acrid taste with some bitterness. [1] `F 5-8`

Sea-Kale - *Crambe maritima* ❀

A coastline plant. Eat the young leaves, while stripping older stems of their outer peel before cooking. Cultivated leaf-stalks are frequently light blanched. [3] `F 6-8`

Sea Lettuce - *Ulva lactua* ❀

This bright green seaweed looks very fragile and delicate. It particularly likes habitats where there is a freshwater outlet to the sea and for that reason care needs to be taken when harvesting to make sure such water sources are not contaminated with exotic effluents. The delicate fronds can be sweated until tender, prepared in a similar manner to purple laver, or eaten raw with a marinade.

Self Heal - *Prunella vulgaris* ❀

The flowering plant may be eaten in salads or cooked with vegetable dishes. [3] `F 5-10`

Shepherd's Purse - *Capsella bursa-pastoris* ❀ 🌶 ⚘

The spring leaves of shepherd's purse are used as a cabbage substitute in some corners of the world. It can be used in salads, boiled in salted water, or even stir-fried. Best used before the plant flowers. Use seed pods as pepper, and the roots as ginger, substitutes. [1] `F 2-11 / FR 3-11`

Silverweed - *Potentilla anserina* ⚘

Silverweed is another of the classic famine crops, the fleshy branched roots edible in their raw state but much better when boiled or roasted. In those centuries when times were tough the roasted roots were ground into meal for transformation into bread or a porridge. The plant contains tannin. [3] `F 5-8`

Sneezewort - *Achillea ptarmica* ❀

Sneezewort sometimes found its way into salads where its hot leaves add pep. [3] `F 6-10`

Prickly Sow-thistle / Spiny Milk-thistle - *Sonchus asper*

Remove the prickles and use the reasonably succulent leaves as a pot-herb vegetable or in salads. [1] F 6-10

Smooth Sow-thistle / Milk-thistle - *Sonchus oleraceus*

Another of the edible sow-thistles, available for most of the year and used in Greece as a winter salad. Boil like spinach, or mix with other pot-herbs, or add to soups. Not to be confused with the Milk Thistle proper. [1] F 6-10

Corn/Perennial Sow-thistle/Field Milk-thistle - *Sonchus arvensis*

Yet another sow-thistle the leaves of which can be used as a summer salad vegetable. The leaves become bitter with age. Like all the sow-thistles two changes of cooking water may be needed to remove some bitterness. [3] F 6-10

Sheep's Sorrel - *Rumex acetosella*

The leaves of sheep's sorrel have a sort of tart gooseberry-lemon taste and the plant was once prized as a vegetable. [3] F 5-7

Wild / Common Sorrel - *Rumex acetosa* – WARNING

This is a plant with a long and prized culinary history although, as you will see from the contra-indications below, it must have done irreparable damage to countless people before the nature of the plant was fully understood - the sharp acid taste is down to the presence of oxalic acid.

Mashed with vinegar and sugar it was used as a cold sauce to go with meat, the juice was used as a rennet substitute to curdle milk in cheese-making, it was used to add piquancy to soups, and was used raw or cooked. These still stand true today, just don't eat too much sorrel. So, eat young leaves boiled or raw, and consider wilting them like spinach and mixing with nettles similarly treated. The one other thing that should be mentioned is that if sorrel is over-cooked it goes sludgy, in addition to losing its green colour. [3] F 5-8

Contra-indications - the acid nature of this plant means that it should be avoided by anyone suffering from arthritis, gout or rheumatism; it may also cause dermatitis; and must be eaten sparingly because it can cause kidney damage.

Wood Sorrel - *Oxalis acetosella* – WARNING

Like its larger sorrel named counterparts the wood sorrel contains oxalic acid in its leaves. A little light cooking will remove the acid taste while a small sprinkle of the fresh leaves added to a salad will provide a piquant touch. [3] F 3-5

Contra-indications - do not eat if you suffer from gout or rheumatism. Poisonous in large amounts.

Spignel - *Meum athamanticum* 🌱

An aromatic plant of northern Britain and Scotland the roots of spignel were employed as a spice, with a flavour like melilot. [3] F 6-7

Spring Beauty - *Montia/Claytonia perfiolata* ☘ 🌱

Cook the young leaves like spinach - they contain vitamins A and C. The tubers can be peeled and boiled. [1] F 3-6

Star of Bethlehem ☠ - *Ornithogalum augustifolium* - WARNING 🌱

Contains cardiac glycosides which are poisonous, yet in the 17th century the roots of this plant were roasted and eaten – apparently mixed with honey. Can also cause intestinal problems. The author has not had a chance to try, but thinks slicing, and boiling two or three times to leach out the toxin, might be a possible treatment. Be VERY careful if you experiment. Your choice. [3] F 4-6

Common Stork's Bill - *Erodium cicutarium* ☘

The young leaves may be eaten raw or boiled in salted water. [1] F 4-7

Sweet Cicely - *Myrrhis odorata* ☘ 🌿 🌱

A plant with a very long culinary and herbal history. More common in northern Britain sweet cicely is almost entirely edible - the aniseedy sweet leaves finding their way into stewed fruit dishes, salads, soups, blanched then battered and fried, or on their own boiled as a vegetable; the roots have been used in salads after boiling and are a substitute for parsnips; and the fruits are used in liquers. Truly the common sweet cicely has many uses. [3] F 5-7

Sweet Sedge / Sweet Flag - *Acorus calamus* – WARNING ☘ 🌱

An aromatic and fragrant plant that looks very much like Irises and Yellow Flag – either of which MUST NOT be eaten. The roots were roasted and eaten by the North American Indians, the leaf buds can be added to salads, while Culpepper remarks that the leaves were: *'put into sauce for fish'*. [3] F 5-7

Sycamore / Great Maple - *Acer pseudo-platanus* ∪

There are naturalist purists who believe that the sycamore should be banished from the British landscape, the reason being that the tree is an alien species belonging to the maple family. What better use then, than to extract sap from the pierced trunks of the sycamore tree. The sap has some sugar content and can be made into wine. F4-5 / FR 6-9

Milk Thistle / Wild Artichoke - *Silybum marianum* ☘ ☘ 🌱

Another very versatile plant - also known as the marian thistle - the young spring leaves of which have been said to be *'very wholesome, and exceed other greens in taste'*. The seedlings can be eaten raw in salads, the de-prickled leaves and shoots boiled or baked in pies, the stems too after peeling, soaking and stewing like rhubarb, and finally the roots which are cooked like parsnips and resemble salsify. The receptacle or base of the purple-violet flowers can be prepared and eaten like cultivated artichoke, but is much smaller. [1] [2] F 6-8

Thistles - *Cirsium species* – WARNING ✤

Parts of many of our common thistles [the **spear thistle** - *Cirsium vulgare* and **marsh thistle** - *C. palustre* for example] can be eaten. Remove the prickles and boil the leaves, the roots of younger stemless specimens are edible raw or cooked, and the young peeled stalks can be chopped and boiled in salted water for a few minutes. The stalks become more fibrous, and less palatable, with age. For something different, dig up the roots of first year *cirsium vulgare* plants, boil, then slice and fry, or cook till very tender, dry and ground as a flour additive or substitute. *C. vulgare* [2] F7-10 / *C. palustre* [3] F 7-9 *Note that some thistle species are poisonous.*

Cotton Thistle - *Onopordon acanthium* ✤

Peel and boil the stems then serve buttered. [2] F 7-9

Woolly Thistle - *Carduus eriophorus* ✤

The very young specimens can be eaten in salads. Young stalks, peeled, soaked in water and then boiled or baked in pies. [2] F 7-9

Red Valerian - *Centranthus ruber* ✤ 🌱

The roots of the red valerian sometimes find their way into soups in France. The leaves are bitter and may be best in salads, while they can be boiled as a vegetable. [3] F 6-8

Bitter Vetch - *Lathyrus linifolius* - WARNING 🌱

Be very careful that you identify this plant correctly as various other vetches are poisonous. However, the tuberous, rhizomous roots of this plant were once grown as food in Scotland where it was called *cormeille*. The raw roots, which can also be dried for later use, have been likened to tasting like chestnuts. [3] F 4-7

Violets - *Viola* ✿ ✤ 🌱

As beautiful as they are the more common violet varieties - **sweet violet** [*V. odorata* [3] F 3-4] and **common dog violet** [*V. riviniana* [3] F 4-5] - offer healthy eating. The leaves are rich in vitamin A and the flowers vitamin C. The small leaves and stalks may be cooked or added to a salad, while the chopped root may be cooked too. The flowers are sometimes candied. *The Fen Violet, Viola persicifolia, is protected.*

Wall Lettuce - *Mycelius muralis* ✤

The leaves can be cooked as a vegetable or used in salads. [3] F 7-9 *The very rare Least Lettuce, Lactuta saligna, is protected.*

Water Avens - *Geum rivale* 🌿

People in rural America would make a decoction of the root - which has a similar clove-like fragrance and taste as its cousin herb bennett - add milk and sugar and drink as a beverage. This was known as Indian Chocolate because of the colour rather than the taste. [3] F 5-9

Common Watercress - *Nasturtium officinale* – WARNING ✿

There is a safety concern with watercress revolving round the larvae of the parasitic liver fluke which like the plant and can therefore find their way into humans through consumption of contaminated leaves. Only gather plants which are associated with fast flowing streams, and avoid gathering it in areas of slow moving or stagnant water, and streams running through fields where sheep graze. The older leaves are the most peppery, and to be on the safe side it is worth cooking the leaves of the wild watercress before eating by boiling or stir-frying. [3] F 6-8

Water Crowfoot - *Ranunculus aquatilis* ✿

America's Gosiute indians used the entire plant, boiling it to remove the bitterness. [3] F 5-6

Water Lily - *Nymphaea nelumbo* 🌿

There are lots of different water lillies around and this one appears to be the only one which is generally agreed upon as being edible. The part in question is the tuberous rootstock which was once eaten raw or cooked. Since the roots are bitter a cooking will help remove the bitterness. The stems of *Nymphaea alba* F6-8 were once eaten as delicacy.

Whitebeam [*Sorbus aria*] & Wild Service Tree [*S. torminalis*] 🌱

The berries of the whitebeam are made into a jelly that is served with venison [once the berries have been 'bletted' - that is, stored in a cool dry place until the fruit has almost become rotten]. Can also be dried and ground into a flour and mixed with cereals. The berries of the wild service tree also used to be eaten. *Sorbus torminalis* F 5-6 / FR 9

Whortleberry - *Vaccinum family* 🌱

This family of plants includes the well-known **bilberry** [*V. myrtillus*] and **red whortleberry** [*V. vitis-idaea*] both of which are edible. John Gerard complained of whortleberries: '*The people of Cheshire do eate the blacke wortles in creame and milke... which stop and binde the belly.*' *V. myrtillus* F 4-6 / *V. vitis-idaea* F 6-7

Wild Parsnip - *Pastinaca sativa* - WARNING 🌿

The wild parsnip, like the wild carrot, is really not worth the effort of digging up and preparing - unless you are desperate or fancy a culinary adventure. The roots are straggly and not at all fleshy like the modern cultivars. Your time would be better spent on finding a more succulent wild vegetable, although one old reference refers to the roots as being: '...*long, white, and well tasted.*' Over to you. [2] `F 7-9`

Contra-indication - handling the leaves can bring on photodermic reactions and blistering in bright sunlight.

Willow - *Salix alba* ✤

Although not yet tried by the author the young leaves are apparently not very palatable but can be steamed and boiled. More of a survival food or for experimenting with than something to look forward to, but once eaten by Alaskan indians. Contain vitamin C. `F 4-5`

Winter Cress / Yellow Rocket - *Barbarea vulgaris* ✤

Often eaten in salads the leaves of the winter cress are rich in vitamin C, however they are slightly bitter but a lot less so than dandelion. [2] `F 5-8`

Yarrow / Milfoil - *Achillea millefolium* – WARNING ✤

Finely chopped, the peppery leaves of yarrow are a rather bitter addition to salads but were commonly used for that purpose in the 17th century. [3] `F 6-10`

Contra-indication – avoid consuming large amounts which can cause headaches.

Yellow / Meadow Goat's Beard - *Tragopogon pratensis* ✤ ♀

This is another of the goat's beard family that is edible and is known in France as wild salsify. One old source says of it: '*It is so pleasant in taste, that it may be eaten in the manner of carrots, and other roots at table, but exceeds them in all its qualities.*' The young leaves may be boiled or eaten raw in salads, the young asparagus-ish tasting pre-flowering stalks chopped and boiled like asparagus, and the black skinned sweet-tasting tapering taproots boiled and eaten like parsnips. Interestingly, historically the roots were stored in dry sand [minimizing exposure to air causing discolouration] for use over the winter months. [1] [3] `F 6-7`

Common Yew ☠ - *Taxus baccata* - WARNING

This is another plant that comes with a **severe hazard warning**. The yew is poisonous, yet the one part that can be eaten - most likely as a garnish - is the orange-red pulp surrounding the black seed of its berries. The black seed is fatal if consumed and MUST NOT even be bitten into, while the orange-red fruit aril has an odd texture and a sort of insipid sweetness. Be very careful how you use and handle yew. `F 2-4 / FR 8-9`

A FINAL WORD

Having read about the many wild plants available for eating you must by now realize the importance of identifying them confidently and correctly. If you cannot identify something walk away from it, and certainly never put it in your mouth.

The author saw an extraordinary news report on television a few years ago where a couple had unwittingly picked the lovely looking glossy berries of deadly nightshade and then frozen these for later use. Six months later a pie was lovingly baked and eagerly consumed. Within hours nightmarish hallucinations set in and three days of uncontrollable physical reactions followed which caused the individuals to lay waste to the interior of their home, never mind the vomiting. The couple were 'rescued' after three days when neighbours wondered why the couple had not been seen around their house. To be honest they were lucky to be alive, and it was thought that the deep freezing process had taken the edge off the toxic effects of the nightshade berries. What really stuns is the stupidity of anyone consuming a plant which they know absolutely nothing about and have not checked.

Always use a good botanical Field Guide, preferably two so you can cross-reference any unfamiliar plant that you are considering for eating.

When trying one of the wild plants listed for the first time, try tasting just a small amount of the prepared plant to check your tolerance. If you have any bad or allergic reactions avoid any further consumption.

Never put any plant into your mouth unless absolutely 100% certain of its identification and edibility. Don't even consider 'pretty sure' as an option.

Only gather ingredients from uncontaminated sources and environments.

SUGGESTED FURTHER READING & GUIDES

Field Guide to the Trees & Shrubs of Britain, Michael W Davison, Ed., Readers Digest, 2001

Field Guide to the Wild Flowers of Britain, Michael W Davison, Ed., Readers Digest, 2001

Collins How to Identify Wild Flowers, Christopher Grey-Wilson & Lisa Alderson, HarperCollins, 2000

Kingfisher Guide to the Trees of Britain & Europe, David Sutton, Kingfisher Publications, 2000

Encyclopedia of Wild Flowers, John Akeroyd, Dempsey Parr, 1999

The Wild Plants of the British Isles, Ian Garrard & David Streeter, Midsummer Books, 1998

Collins Complete British Wildlife Photoguide, Paul Sterry, HarperCollins, 1997

Honey from a Weed, Patience Gray, Lyons & Burnford, NY, 1997

Kingfisher Guide to Wild Flowers of Britain & Northern Europe, David Sutton, Kingfisher Publications, 1996

Encyclopaedia of Herbs and Herbalism, Malcolm Stuart, Ed., Caxton/Macdonald & Co., 1989

US Army Field Manual FM21-76 – Survival, Unites States Army, 1970

A Modern Herbal, Mrs M Grieve, Harcourt, Brace & Company, 1931

Ethnobotany of the Menomini Indians, Huron H Smith, Mus. of City of Milwaukee, 1923 *[online]*

Useful Wild Plants of the United States & Canada, Charles Francis Saunders, Robert McBride & Co., New York, 1920 *[online]*

The Wild Foods of Great Britain, L. Cameron, Geo. Routledge & Sons, 1917

The Ethnobotany of the Gosiute Indians of Utah, Ralph V Chamberlin, American Anthropological Assoc., c1912 *[online]*

Ethnobotany of the Zuni Indians, Matilda Stevenson, Bureau of American Ethnology, 1908-9 *[online]*

The Compleat Angler, Izzak Walton, 1653 *[online]*

The English Physitian, Nicholas Culpepper, 1652 *[online]*

The Herball or General Historie of Plantes, John Gerard, 1633 *[online]*

THE RECIPES

The 240-odd recipes in the following section are not about 'presentation' but about providing no-fuss food with interesting taste combinations and to inspire experimentation. Where possible the recipes try to be simple in their construction and execution, and try not to require the preparer to have a degree in rocket science. After all, Gas Mark 7 and 425° mean very little when you are on the moors and only have a frying pan and cooking pot – or even less. The same also goes for measuring ingredients. Where possible these are given in quantities which can be mentally visualized without the need for kitchen scales. The quantities can be simply amended according to your own personal taste.

The recipes mostly presume you don't have whizzers, kitchen gadgets, time or space to make pastry, fine temperature control ovens (but rather simple ones with low, medium and high settings). In any case, many of the recipes could be adapted as casseroles, for cooking over a fire, or wrapping in foil and broiling or baking in embers. As long as the food is cooked through - and hopefully not burnt by such treatment - it is imagined most outdoors cooks will welcome hot food rather than worry about gastronomic niceties and culinary technique.

On a similar topic, the recipes frequently specify butter and/or oil in the knowledge that many readers cooking outdoors will be limited in what they have – perhaps only a packet of all-purpose lard! If you're not a knowledgeable foodie then consider using light oils like rapeseed, sunflower and corn oil for general frying and deep-frying. Chinese style stir-frying is best with oils like groundnut and corn oil, or sesame for more authenticity. And you might want to use peanut, hazel or walnut oils for unusual salad dressings. Keep much thicker olive oil for special dressings and those meals requiring a touch of class.

The recipes do allow for the odd additional luxury that the outdoors person might be able to carry with them - a squirreled away bottle of soy sauce, that tube of tomato paste, chunk of root ginger, an onion, block of creamed coconut, dried prawns for fish flavouring, or sachets of favourite dried herbs and spices. The bottom line is that these luxuries aren't too bulky or heavy to carry. Readers with a caravan or narrowboat will be better able to carry additional supplies and also perform more complex cooking methods. As for those cooking at home... well you will have every opportunity to elaborate on the recipes with carrots, bacon, peas and all the many everyday foodstuffs that we take for granted – thanks to 24/7 supermarket shopping.

For anyone really hard-pressed to conjure up food in the wild, then you can always take a leaf out of the old cookbooks and boil your game fowl or rabbit. Although that might sound rather dull it was quite common during the 16th century for meat to be boiled, with mace, currants, dates and blackberries added to the boiling water to provide flavour and sweetness. There were also exotic stuffings; gooseberry and grape stuffed roast chicken, for example. Carp could be cooked with currants and prunes.

Even earlier recipes recommended cod and haddock cooked with figs, raisins and wine, and whelks boiled in ale before pickling. Over to you, and your sense of adventure... It could be a blue cheese - like stilton - with venison, a spicy port sauce to go with pigeon, or some sort of creamed wild vegetable.

With 'wild foods' you are cooking the unconventional and are also dependent on what your immediate 'natural larder' has to offer. A location will not necessarily provide all the ingredients you need at the same time, so unless a meal is a matter of survival sustenance adopt a frame of mind willing to adapt and push forward the boundaries of tastes and textures. Do not be afraid to step outside the realm of traditional kitchen cookbook foods - experiment. You will no doubt have the odd disastrous mix of flavours from time to time, but then all pioneers expect to have a setback along the way - or even get shot at by injuns.

As your knowledge of wild ingredients widens you will be able to take control of the tastes and textures that you personally enjoy but, above all, explore them. Hopefully you will find that food produced from wild resources does not have to be dull or mundane.

Only eat the wild plant parts recommended. Just because the leaves of a plant are edible that does not mean the roots or flowers are, and vice versa. Where you see the asterisk '*' symbol you should check on the potential medical complications and hazards with the plant. Wherever you are unfamiliar with a wild plant ingredient check back with the *plant reference section* to get to know about the background and preparation details. Once you become familiar with all the various foodstuffs to be found in the wild you will be able to mix and substitute ingredients within the recipes.

Wild ingredients should only be harvested from safe stocks. Don't use roadside plants, or those near landfill sites, evil looking lagoons and stagnant water, or from fields and neighbouring borders that may have recently been sprayed with chemicals. Look for signs of chemical deposits on leaves, or wilted plants. Agricultural herbicides are often selective, so you may find all the thistles in a field are wilted, but the rest of the greenery looks lush and inviting. It won't be. The same goes for any small game you acquire. Look for signs of any poisoning, particularly in forest areas where poisoned bait may have been laid down for squirrels. Certainly never eat any dead animal that you find lying on the ground. Something killed it – a disease, old age or poison – and it may well have been poisoned.

It goes without saying that - depending on what you are using - the recipes assume the component ingredients have been washed, gutted, dressed, cleaned or peeled ready for use, and are bug and disease free.

So, be prepared to leave behind those frozen peas, burgers and pizzas. Cast off your inhibitions and enter the world of ***Really* Wild** food.

FURTHER THOUGHTS

SCALING & PREPARING WILD FISH

While the gutting and beheading process are somewhat obvious, removing the scales [which can be very tough with a fish like Perch] may be something rather more daunting.

Since the outdoors person isn't likely to carry one of the fangled gadgets for removing scales, or even a wire brush which is sometimes employed, the simplest way is to plunge the fish into boiling water for a few seconds and then scrape the scales off. Doing the scraping under water can make the process much less messy.

If your fish is going to be baked whole or poached - as opposed to the requirement for fish fillets - make your life easy and leave the skin and scales on, and remove these after cooking. Then, with the fish lying flat, simply skin the cooked meat to reveal the tasty treat awaiting.

If you are cooking a fish with the skin and scales intact make sure to clean the exterior properly. Carp, for example, can be quite slimy and tench particularly so.

DE-MUDDYING WILD FISH

Some freshwater fish, particularly those found in lakes and muddy rivers may taste 'muddy' and this can be partly dealt with by washing the gutted fish well and also soaking in water acidified with some vinegar - 1 tablespoon of vinegar and a pinch of salt to each pint of water.

If you have the luxury of catching a live fish and have space, then consider placing your catch in clean fresh water and allowing it to swim for several hours or overnight.

FINDING & PREPARING WILD SHELLFISH

Recipes for scallops and razor shells are included in the guide. While scallops tend to be found in offshore low tide shallows, and are therefore not always easily harvested by the amateur, *razor shell clams* are much easier to acquire. They can be found in the soft low tide sand and reveal their potential location with little dimples in the sand about the size of a thumb print. Pour salt into the hole and wait for the razor to emerge. Grab hold of the shell tightly and pull hard to dislodge its grip from the sand. Note, however, that the razor is sensitive to vibration so you will need to tread softly along the sand.

In the case of **scallops** it is likely that you will buy these from a local fisherman rather than collect them yourself as the scallops are found further out in the shallows. The knack to opening scallops is to place the unopened beasties on top of a warm cooker or steam them open in a pan. Once inside remove the frilly brown and black bits but keep the fleshy white and orange-pink coral parts. Voila, you have one scallop to prepare as you will.

Another shellfish worthy of attention is the **periwinkle** with their little snail-like shell and which can be collected from low-water shoreline rocks. Before using they should have impurities removed by soaking for several hours in salted water. They can be steamed for about 5 minutes or boiled in water laced with herbs. Use a pin to 'winkle' out your winkles, and discard the 'door' and the last few millimetres of the emerging mollusc.

Limpets are another rock-clinging sea mollusc and can be prised from the rocks with a knife, or by giving the shell a quick rap with a stone or coin which shocks the limpet into slackening its hold on the rock. Limpets can be tough. Soak in fresh water and then either steam until the meat loosens or bring to the boil in a pan of water until they emerge from their shells.

Cockles bury themselves under the sand and are harvested at low tide. To purge of possible impurities wash them in fresh water then soak in salted water for several hours, finally giving another rinse. Steam cockles open as with scallops and use the meat as required.

In all cases these shellfish should be harvested in places that are well away from human settlements and potential man-made polluting effluents; one reason for not including the wild water-filtering mussel which can give a nasty dose of food poisoning. And that is something you do not want if you are days from civilization. For safety, don't eat any of the shellfish raw.

WHEN IS *WILD* GAME FOWL COOKED?

The same sort of cautions apply to cooking game fowl as when cooking chicken - cook to the bone, as the saying goes. When baking or roasting a game bird if you insert the tip of a knife into the thigh or breast the juices running out should be clear. A pinkish tinge demands extra cooking. And if you do ever come across raw meat then it isn't 100% safe. If the meat has just come from the cooking process then it's fine to carry on cooking, but otherwise the same rules apply to the re-heating any meat that has cooled or chilled. Incidentally, when working out portions allow a minimum of one pigeon per person as they are small and do not have much meat.

HANGING W̷N̷ GAME

What is 'hanging' game all about? Well game meat generally improves in tenderness and flavour if it is allowed to 'hang' in a cool, well ventilated place for a few days. What happens is that after the initial rigor mortis occurs in the animal its muscle tissue begins to break down and thereby the tenderizing process starts. If you think about it logically, game animals have been flapping and running round the countryside all their life and have well exercised and developed muscle tissue – like a well-honed athlete - unlike flabby battery-reared chickens [vis. your average couch potato]. Hanging therefore softens the muscle tissue.

Hanging also allows the blood to drain out the muscle; rabbits are hung by their legs and game fowl by their necks. Don't skin or pluck the animals before hanging.

The duration of the hanging period is an imprecise art – the idea is not to let the meat *rot* but just tenderize. While a pigeon may benefit from a couple of days, larger and older birds – pheasant say – may want four or five days hanging. Animals like deer may need 2-3 weeks. When a carcass is hung for an extended period it is said to be 'well hung' or 'high', and some connoisseurs of game like their meat so 'high' that it can almost walk out of a room on its own. In that case it is sometimes not pleasant to eat.

W̷N̷ RABBIT WARNINGS

A number of recipes in the guide use rabbit - look upon this as your participation in reducing the rabbit over-population [similarly with pigeons]. However, rabbits can carry a health warning for those preparing the meat....

Apart from avoiding the consumption of any rabbit you find with the awful looking myxomitosis virus the other disease to watch out for is *tularemia* which can be transmitted to humans through skin contact. If you are skinning a rabbit it is therefore best to wear gloves.

A visual way for checking whether a rabbit has tularemia is to look for white or yellow blotches on its liver. If the rabbit you are dressing shows such signs, discard it and find something else to eat.

W̷N̷ CONDIMENTS & FLAVOURINGS

In the absence of the usual condiments and spices, a number of wild plants can offer partial substitutes, but *not* a great many alternatives.

The dried seeds of charlock can stand in for mustard and shepherd's purse root for a basic ginger substitute. Use dried lovage root as a pepper substitute, and herb bennet root instead of cloves. While the seeds of alexanders, and dried barberry and juniper berries can also be used for flavouring, and ramsons can partially offer a garlic flavour.

ᚹᚾᚢᚨ THICKENERS

Flour and cornflour are really the simplest thickeners that outdoor cooks can carry with them, but in the absence of these there other ways of thickening soups and sauces.

The tubers of arrowhead, bullrushes and reeds, roots of silverweed and bistort, all contain starch in some extractable form or other. One of the most abundant sources, apart from bullrush roots, are the well baked roots of the arum or cuckoopint, but since this plant is highly toxic unless treated correctly you really need to be confident about handling it. If you have some 'prepared' acorns then a mash of these can also be used to thicken up stews. Ground hazelnuts, too, can be used for thickening.

Incidentally, the author read on a permaculture website some time ago that acre for acre a crop of bullrushes may produce more starch than maize.

ᚹᚾᚢᚨ FLOURS

Many of wild flour substitutes - acorn, buckwheat, chestnut, for example - contain little, or absolutely no, gluten content. In those recipes for biscuit-type foods it is therefore necessary to add some means of holding things together. For some recipes adding 10 or 20% plain flour will provide enough binding. Another alternative is to mix egg with the ingredients as a binder. Incidentally, for all the recipes in the guide that simply specify 'flour' as an ingredient, this refers to the plain wheat flour variety for simplicity.

CARBOHYDRATE IN THE ᚹᚾᚢᚨ

Many of the recipes in this guide, such as stews, have potatoes among their ingredients. However, carrying heavy water-laden potatoes around the countryside in quantity is not exactly practical. And unless there are plentiful supplies of water, and the time available for pre-soaking, then pulses such as kidney beans and chickpeas are really out of the question. Dried pasta is an option but it is generally rather brittle, and pulverized tagliatelli or macaroni won't look nearly as appetizing as when the real thing is served up in your local Italian cafe. Acorn and chestnut pastas are possible as you will discover.

Although they need water for cooking and re-hydration there are a number of other alternatives which provide carbohydrate but with a reduced weight overhead, and also take up less volume than shaped pasta:

Couscous - this has to be one of the simplest options, needing little more than boiling water poured over the grains and then allowed to swell for a few minutes [couscous can also be steamed for about 40-45 minutes].

Egg noodles - depending on their thickness dried egg noodles can be ready in about 5 minutes, although the dried noodles are fragile and the same thoughts about handling pasta also apply.

Rice - the recipes in this guide presume that you use the popular quick-cook long grain rice, which can be cooked 2 measures of water to one of rice - allowing just enough water to cook and re-hydrate the rice while keeping the goodness of the starch content.

Red & Green Lentils - these take longer to cook but also offer a valuable and different alternative to rice and potatoes, and do not need soaking before cooking.

Polenta - a staple based in Italian cooking which uses finely ground corn meal cooked in boiling water and then simmered for anything from 20-45 minutes.

Some of the recipes here call for breadcrumbs and meal, and rather than carry these with you it is worth considering carrying rolled oats or porridge oats as an alternative. Although these may need further crushing when used as meal the oats will certainly have more nutritional value than breadcrumbs, while they also provide you with the option of porridge on a cold morning should you so decide.

TIPS ON DRYING WILD LEAVES AND HERBS

Select the best leaves you can - without decay or discolouration - and do so on a dry day. Depending on whether the leaf is succulent or not you may need to use additional heat sources to help the drying process. In every case the heat applied should not be too hot - you are not trying to cook the leaves, merely drive the water out from them. Seasoned collectors even have 'dessicators' at their disposal.

Without such equipment you can simply place the leaves on a rack or porous screen so that the air can get at them. Alternatively, if you are into serious 'serial' drying, tie bunches of leaves or stalks and hang from a peg, or length of string.

The bottom line is to allow warm air to circulate round the herbs and leaves, without exposing them to direct sunlight - which can get too hot and consequently drive off some of the aromatic essences of the plant. If the worst comes to the worst you may need to put the leaves into a warm oven - at a very low setting.

When the leaves have become brittle then they are ready to be stored in airtight containers. Store in the dark, and try to keep the leaves as whole as possible until the time you need to use them for cooking.

Roots need to be dried in an oven set at about 50-60°C - technically a 'slow' oven. Remove side shoots, wash and pat dry. Cut into sections, and if thick slice lengthwise to speed drying. Liquorice and marsh mallow roots should be peeled before drying.

For seeds, collect when dry and spread out on paper in an airy place. The drying process may take 2-3 weeks.

When trying one of the wild plants listed for the first time, try tasting just a small amount of the prepared plant to check your tolerance. If you have any bad or allergic reactions avoid any further consumption.

Never put any plant into your mouth unless absolutely 100% certain of its identification and edibility. Don't even consider 'pretty sure' as an option.

Only gather ingredients from uncontaminated sources and environments.

MEATY THINGS

RABBIT KIEV

Rabbit fillets / pieces
Ramsons leaves
Butter
Salt and pepper
Flour
1 egg - beaten
Breadcrumbs
Oil

Yes, believe it! You heard it here first. This is an adaptation of the classic Chicken Kiev using ramsons to provide a replacement for the traditional garlic flavouring – although they lose much of their flavour with cooking. You will only get fillets from a very large rabbit, so for smaller animals cut what meat there is into the largest possible boneless pieces.

• Begin by placing the rabbit fillets on a flat surface and from one end make a cavity in the fillet using a long sharp knife. • Take a couple of the long spear-like ramsons leaves, fold lengthwise a couple of times and then insert into the cavity. • Push a sliver of soft butter inside too and squeeze gently to force some along the length of the fillet.

• Roll the fillets in flour, then dip into beaten egg and roll in fresh breadcrumbs [or meal], if necessary pressing them so the coating sticks. • All that remains to do is fry in oil at a quite high temperature for about 5-8 minutes each side until nicely browned [Chicken Kiev is usually deep fried, however that cooking method is not always practicable when outdoors]. • If there is a bit of wood sorrel or ordinary sorrel in your vicinity it might be worth making a little sauce and trying it as an accompaniment.

RABBIT GOULASH

Rabbit meat - cubed
Onions
Tomatoes
Butter or oil
Paprika
Stock
Salt and pepper

Ingredient measurements here are kept minimal so that you can adapt according to your circumstances. However, you should consider using approximately a good pinch of paprika to every cup of meat, and a couple of tomatoes per person. But then it's all down to a matter of personal taste.

• Roughly chop a couple of onions and sauté in a heavy bottomed pan along with the rabbit meat until nicely browned. • Reduce to a very low heat. • Add seasoning and paprika, and stir thoroughly. • Quarter the tomatoes [skin if you wish] and layer these over the rabbit meat. • Add enough stock - vegetable or chicken - to just cover the pan ingredients. • Cover and continue cooking at a very oh-so-slow gentle simmer for about an hour.

VARIATIONS
If you have some sour cream available try stirring a little of this into the goulash before serving.

SPICED RABBIT MEATBALLS

½ cup red lentils
2 hard-boiled eggs
2 cups minced / finely chopped rabbit
1 egg
1 small onion
Lemon juice
Salt, pepper, cinnamon and nutmeg

• Cook the lentils in water until they are soft and can be mashed, and prepare the two hard-boiled eggs and shell.

• Place the rabbit meat in a bowl and add a raw egg, the onion finely chopped, a splash of lemon juice, spices and pinches of seasoning. • Strain the lentils, mash and add to the meat. • Mix everything together well.

• The mixture should be divided into two and then formed round the hard-boiled eggs to create two quite large meatballs - a bit like Scotch eggs. • Put these onto a greased dish and bake in an oven for 30 minutes in a moderate oven, or until cooked. They could also be deep-fried.

RABBIT & PIGEON KEBAB

Rabbit meat and pigeon breast
Oil
Lemon juice
Paprika and oregano
Salt and pepper

For those with a passion for some Greek, Stavros has set up shop in the wild...

• Marinade the meat in a mixture of the oil, oregano, paprika and lemon juice - preferably for several hours. • Then place the meat on skewers spaced with other vegetables to hand. • Before cooking over a barbeque, or in a frying pan, season your kebabs. Serve with any combination of rice or salad you choose.

VARIATIONS
If you want something more garlicky replace the paprika with chopped ramsons or hedge garlic [ramsons loose much of their garlic properties on cooking]. Another option thought about is to purée some raw damsons or crab-apples and use the acid juice of these instead of the lemon, but it would probably need something sweet adding to the mixture - perhaps some honey or maple syrup - and also eliminating the paprika in the seasoning. You can always kebab vension too.

RABBITBURGERS, DUCKBURGERS & OTHERBURGERS

2-3 cups ground or minced meat
1 finely chopped small onion
1 egg
1-2 slices bread, crumbed
Salt, pepper, oregano, chopped ramsons
Butter or oil

Here's one for fast food addicts, though you'll have to catch your meal first.

• Mix the meat, onion, egg and crumbed bread together well, then form them into burger sized patties. • You can roll them in breadcrumbs if you wish, but you might prefer to fry straight in butter or oil.

Meats like rabbit and pigeon have very little fat with their flesh so it's important not to overcook them as they will possibly become very dry. Duck has body fat which can be incorporated into the ground meat to add moisture, while goose is very fatty and will need some removing. The addition of some chopped greens within the meat mixture can also supply extra moisture to a very lean meat like rabbit which may dry out in the cooking process.

RABBIT HASH BROWNS

Potatoes
Rabbit meat
Butter
Salt and pepper

Hash Browns hail from America originally and this adaptation replaces the traditional bacon or ham content with rabbit; an important difference because it means there is vastly less salt in this recipe and little fat on the meat.

• Boil the potatoes until they can just be pierced with a fork, but don't overcook. • Remove from the heat, drain off the water and allow to cool. • Then dice the potatoes into small ½-inch, sugar lump-sized cubes.

• Meanwhile you can have been cooking the rabbit meat, which should have been stripped off the bone, chopped and fried in butter until it browns slightly. • Remove sautéd rabbit meat from the pan and set aside. • With the heat turned high spread the diced potato evenly across the bottom of the pan and then add the rabbit meat. • Add seasoning [if you like the saltiness of traditional hash then make sure to season well], then press down on the mixture with a slice. The idea is to get the potato on the bottom of the pan to start producing a lovely golden crust, but for this not to stick to the bottom surface. So give the pan a shake occasionally, or think about using a non-stick pan.

• Continue cooking for about 15-20 minutes with the heat reduced, checking occasionally how bottom browning in progressing. If necessary extend the cooking time. • To serve, cut into slices with your slice and flip sunny side up as you place it on the plate. If you really want to impress your friends place an inverted serving dish over the frying pan and flip over.

SPICY RABBIT STEW

Rabbit - jointed	Sugar
Vinegar & wine	Salt and pepper
Butter or oil	Bay leaves
2 onions	Cloves [or herb bennett root]
½ cup flour	

This recipe requires an overnight marinade of the rabbit, but then you might just be sleeping. Or perhaps not.

• Joint the rabbit into pieces and then marinate overnight in wine and vinegar - about 1 cup of vinegar to 3 of wine. • Drain but keep the marinade. • To cook, melt a couple of tablespoons of butter in a pan big enough to hold all the rabbit pieces. • Sauté the rabbit for about 10-15 minutes then set aside.

• Slice the onions and sauté in a second pan with more butter, then stir the flour into the softened onions. • Add the marinade to the pan and continue stirring over the heat until a smooth sauce develops. • Pop in the rabbit pieces and any butter remaining in the frying pan. • Add a good pinch of sugar, seasoning, a couple of bay leaves, and a few cloves. • Cover, turn the heat down low, and simmer gently for 45-50 minutes or until the rabbit is tender. • Add a little water from time to time if the liquid looks as if it may be drying.

RABBIT STEW - 2

1 rabbit	1 potatoes - 1 per person
Bacon	1 garlic clove
Butter or oil	Herbs
2 pints chicken stock / water	Salt and pepper
2 onions	

• Cut the rabbit into portions, chop the onions into chunks, and cube the potatoes. • In a deep pan fry the bacon until it is very well done and most of the fat has been cooked out. • Remove bacon from the pan and set aside. • Fry the rabbit portions in the residual bacon fat till lightly browned all over.

• Add the chicken stock [use more water or stock if feeding several people], bring to the boil then simmer for about 30 minutes. • Add the vegetables, herbs, and the finely chopped garlic. • Simmer for about 20 more minutes or until the vegetables are cooked. • Add seasoning to taste. • Serve with the well fried bacon broken into the stew.

VARIATIONS
You might like to try ham as a replacement for bacon, but this will require frying off the rabbit pieces in butter or oil first. The addition of some tomatoes would add a sweetness to the stew.

STIR-FRIED RABBIT & BURDOCK

Burdock root	Rabbit meat
1 small onion	Butter or oil
Ginger - root preferred	Salt and pepper
Soy sauce	
Honey - or sugar	
Sesame oil - preferred	

The idea behind this recipe is to bring a touch of the Japanese way of using burdock - they call it gobo - with rather more mundane rabbit. It is a method which takes some time and the recipe recognizes that you may not be able to get your hands on some ingredients.

• Begin by peeling the burdock root and then cutting into julienne strips [that's like a 2-2½ inch matchstick]. • Soak for about an hour in water. • Nearer the time, finely chop a small onion and grate a bit of ginger and place in a pan in readiness for the burdock root.

• Meanwhile, quickly stir-fry some diced rabbit meat, season, set aside and keep warm. • Drain your burdock juliennes thoroughly. • Put some sesame oil [this provides an oriental touch, but other oils will do] in a pan and turn the heat up high. • Soften the chopped onion and then add the burdock and fry for several minutes - stirring to keep the pieces moving. • Add the ginger, soy sauce and honey and cook for a few minutes more. • Serve the rabbit pieces on top of portions of your oriental burdock.

SWEET & SOUR RABBIT

Rabbit meat	Tomato purée
Salt and pepper	Soy sauce
1 egg	Vinegar
Flour	Brown sugar
Butter or oil	Cornflour
Onion	Water
Garlic	

Your local take-away will never seem quite the same after this one...

• Dice the rabbit meat into big pieces, dip pieces into beaten egg and then into the flour. • Fry the meat in oil or butter until it is nicely browned all over. • Remove and set aside.

• Chop the onion and garlic and fry in the pan for 5 minutes or until they soften. • Add a good squidge of tomato purée, good slugs of soy sauce and vinegar, a tablespoon of sugar, and several good pinches of cornflour which has been mixed in some water. • Boil and cook for three minutes, making sure to stir so the sauce is smooth, then combine the fried rabbit meat and reduce the heat. • Cook for a few minutes more, and simmer for about 10 minutes depending on how large the chunks of meat are.

VARIATIONS
The tomato purée can be replaced by tomato sauce ·if that is the only thing available to you, and the sugar can be white.

BRAISED RED WINE RABBIT

1 rabbit	1 garlic clove
Oil	Tomato purée [optional]
2 cups mushrooms	Salt and pepper
2-3 small onions	Thyme
1-2 cups red wine	
½ cup chicken stock	

• Cut the rabbit into portions and season. • Halve the onions lengthwise, and also the mushrooms if they are large. • Heat the oil in a casserole or heavy pan and brown the rabbit pieces. Keep the meat moving in the pan so that it does not stick. • Pour off the remaining oil, then add the onions, whole garlic clove [crush or slice if you want a more than a hint of the garlic], and mushrooms.

• Cook for about 5 minutes, keeping all the ingredients moving. • Add the chicken stock, a small squidge of tomato paste if you wish, plus the red wine and some thyme. • Bring the contents of the pan to the boil then reduce the heat, cover, and simmer until the rabbit is tender - about 30-40 minutes.

CIDER RABBIT STEW

Rabbit - jointed
Plums
1 pint cider
2 or 3 small onions
2 tsp. mustard
½ pint water
2 tbsp. flour
Salt and pepper
Butter or oil
Wild rootstock - sweet cicely, arrowhead, bullrush

Don't be so mean! Share that cider of yours with a rabbit...

• Slice the onions, pierce the plums with a fork and place in a bowl along with the cider, water, mustard and rabbit joints. • Marinade for several hours, or preferably overnight.

• Remove rabbit from marinade, dry off then sauté in some butter until browned. • Place the rabbit pieces in a casserole [or heavy bottomed pan if you have no oven]. • Add the marinade ingredients - with the exception of the plums - the chopped rootstock of choice, mustard and seasoning. • Mix the flour with a little of the marinade liquor and stir into the casserole. • Bring to the boil to develop the sauce, cover, then place in a moderate pre-heated oven and bake for about 30-40 minutes - or simmer for the equivalent time or until tender.

• The plums are the last item to be added and cooking time will vary on ripeness. • The whole cooking time should be about 60 minutes, or until done, so if the plums are very ripe then they can be added 10 minutes before the end, if firm then more like 20 minutes.

RABBIT & RICE WITH NETTLES

2-3 cups minced rabbit meat
Butter or oil
Salt, pepper, cinnamon & paprika
1 pint of young nettle leaves
1 cup water
1 medium onion
Butter or oil
1 egg
1½-2 cups partly cooked rice

• Gently fry the seasoned rabbit meat in some butter or oil until nicely browned then set aside. • Wash the nettle leaves and boil gently until tender in half a cup of water.

• Chop the onion and also fry. • When beginning to soften add some of the water from the greens before finally adding the leaves themselves to the pan. • Stir in and cook for a couple of minutes, then remove from the heat.

• Beat the egg in a bowl and add 2 or 3 tablespoons of the partly cooked rice. • Place the egged rice at the bottom of a small baking dish, the nettle leaves and onions evenly on top, and the rabbit meat over this. Top everything with the remainder of the rice. • Cover and place in a medium oven for 10-15 minutes, before reducing to a low heat and cooking for another 20-30 minutes. What you should end up with is crispy golden rice on the bottom and fluffy white rice above.

ALTERNATIVES
Try adding a bit of saffron to the rabbit fry-up stage or even turmeric. And optionally you can add the fried leaves and onions to some yoghurt and add seasoning before turning them into the baking dish.

LOVAGE & RABBIT SAUCE

2 cups diced rabbit	1 cup diced lovage* stems
Butter or oil	Butter or oil
Large onion	Lemon juice [or sorrel infused water]
Pinches of salt and pepper	Nutmeg
1 cup water	

• Fry the rabbit meat and onions till brown, adding seasoning. • Add a cup of water to this, cover, and cook for a further 10-15 minutes or until the meat is tender.

• In a second pan sauté the chopped celery-like lovage in butter or oil for about 10 minutes. • Add these to the simmered meat, along with a couple of good slugs of lemon juice and simmer for a further 10-15 minutes. Serve with rice or couscous.

STEAMED RABBIT

Rabbit meat
Mushrooms
Water
Ginger [root preferred]
Spring onion [optional]
Salt and pepper

• Cut off-the-bone rabbit meat into thin slices, put in a basin with a pinch of salt and pepper, a couple of small slices of ginger [or a pinch of ginger powder] and place in a steamer for about 10 minutes. • Then add a cup of water, several sliced mushrooms and stir. • Raise the heat and steam for about another 20 minutes. This Chinese influenced dish can be served with rice, and consider steaming some shredded and soaked burdock root alongside the meat.

RABBIT SATAY

Rabbit meat
Garlic clove
Ginger - grated root preferred
Soy sauce
Clear honey
Oil
Japanese knotweed stems [or sliced lemon grass]

Lest thine eyes covet thy neighbour's back garden... although it should be said that countless millions of people in less well off countries rear rabbits for the pot. A sort of domesticus bunnicus for the masses, and for whom a spot of curried paw is as welcome as a date and apple sandwich or a wopperburger.

True satay is generally served with a peanut sauce, but since this is an unlikely resource in the wild it has been left out. On the other hand you can make an interesting hazelnut equivalent by cooking ground hazels in creamed coconut and then sweetening. In their absence you could serve with a toffee type sweet dip made by melting a little brown sugar and adding a few drops of vinegar.

• Cut the meat into cubes and set aside. • Meanwhile put crushed garlic, grated ginger, a slug of soy sauce, about a tablespoon of clear honey and a little oil into a small bowl and mix together. • Take a handful of knotweed stems, bruise and place in the bottom of a larger bowl. • Add the meat and marinade then mix to ensure the meat is coated. • Leave for several hours. • Skewer the meat and grill or cook over a fire until done.

THAI-STYLE RABBIT SOUP

2 cups rabbit meat - chopped	2 tbsp. coconut cream
1 garlic clove	2 tbsp. peanut butter
Butter or oil	1 lemon [lime preferred] - juiced
Turmeric – good pinch	Spring onion
Chilli powder – pinch	Salt and pepper
1 pint chicken stock	

A touch of 'The Rabbit and I' starring... more ingredients than many outdoors people will carry with them... So this recipe is for readers at home wondering what to do with those unused bits of rabbit meat.

• Chop the garlic finely and fry until it begins to colour. • Add the chopped rabbit meat to the pan, then stir. • Add in the spices and stir-fry for several more minutes.

• Meanwhile, crumble and dissolve the coconut into hot chicken stock. • Add to the pan along with peanut butter and lemon juice. • Stir everything together thoroughly, turn down the heat to a gentle simmer and cover. • Cook for about 15-20 minutes then add chopped spring onion and seasoning. • Allow to cook for another 5 minutes. Serve.

VARIATIONS
In the absence of peanut butter why not try ground hazelnuts which will also act as a thickener? And if you have some dried egg noodles, consider adding a handful or two when adding the chicken stock - add an extra ½-1 cup of water to allow for absorbtion by the noodles.

MUSTARD POTATOES & SAUSAGE

Potatoes - or arrowhead roots
Spicy sausages
Mustard greens or seedlings
Butter
1 cup stock [vegetable or chicken]
Salt and pepper

This is one of the times that you are permitted a luxury from beyond the world of wild food - sausages. They can be an ordinary vanilla brand but you would be much better off with one of the premium or spiced sausages - perhaps a Spanish chorizo type. Down to you.

• Peel and then boil some potatoes until they soften, then slice and place in an oven dish. • While the potatoes are boiling pan-fry or grill the sausages till done and then slice into chunks [or keep whole depending on whether it's a 'fork' meal or a full set of spanners affair]. • Mix the sausage chunks with the potatoes in the oven dish.

• Meanwhile, take a large knob of butter and wilt some young mustard greens or seedlings of either the black or white mustard plant. • Remove from the heat and spread the greens over the contents of the oven dish. • Into the remaining butter blend a couple of good pinches of flour, stir in the stock and then pour over the potatoes and sausages. • Place in a hot oven or cook under the grill for another 5-10 minutes.

VARIATIONS
The vegetable part of this recipe can form a dish in its own right. And ready-mixed mustard could be used.

ELDERBERRY & GAME SAUCE

2 cups cubed game meat
Large onion
Butter or oil
Salt, pepper, nutmeg and cinnamon
2 cups water
1 ½ tbsp. lemon juice
1-2 cups dried elderberries

• Gently fry the meat, finely chopped onion and seasoning. • Then add the water and lemon juice and simmer gently for about 30 minutes. • Add the dried elderberries and continue to simmer for another 10-15 minutes or until they begin to soften. • Season further if required. Best served with rice.

BACON & MUSTARD GREENS

Bacon
1 pint mustard greens
Water
Oil or butter

• Fry bacon until quite crisp, then remove from the pan and set aside. • Meanwhile, boil de-stemmed leaves for a couple of minutes then drain. • Put a little more oil or butter in the frying pan, raise the heat and add the mustard greens. • Cook for a few minutes, stirring to make sure the greens don't burn. • Remove from the heat. • Simply break the bacon into pieces, sprinkle over the mustard greens and toss with a fork. Serve.

MAPLE GAME STEW

3-4 cups game meat
Butter or oil
Maple syrup or honey
4 cups water
3 onions
Turnips or other wild rootstock
Potatoes
Green stem vegetable
Salt and pepper

This recipe will work best with larger game like deer, but lean beef could substitute. • Brown chunkily diced meat in some oil or butter then place in a large pan. • Meanwhile slice the onions, dice turnips [or other 'prepared' wild rootstock] and potatoes, and slice a stem vegetable [leek, celery or a prepared wild substitute].

• Add the vegetables to the pan, with the water plus 2-3 tablespoons of maple syrup, or 2 tablespoons of honey, and seasoning. • Simmer over a low to medium heat for about an hour or until the meat is tender.

MEATBALL & DRIED FRUIT SOUP

1 cup of ground meat	Dried elderberries
2 small finely chopped onions	Dried fruit [ie. apricots]
Pinches of cinnamon, pepper, salt	Chopped nuts [walnuts or hazelnuts]
4 cups water	Vinegar
Handful of rice	Sugar
Butter or oil	Pinches of cinnamon and pepper

• Start the rice going, putting the water in a pan and adding the rice, plus a pinch of salt. • Cook gently for 10 minutes.

• Meanwhile, get on with making the meatballs - mixing the meat, one of the finely chopped onions and seasoning thoroughly. • Roll into small balls and lightly fry.

• Add a handful of dried elderberries to the rice pan and continue cooking.
• Lightly fry the second onion and set aside.

• Take your meatballs, handful of other dried fruits [if you are using] and nuts, and the fried onion and add to the rice. • Cook for a further 15 minutes on a medium heat before adding slugs of vinegar and sugar. • Cook 5 minutes more. • In the last few moments stir in pinches of cinnamon and pepper.

ACORN MEATLOAF

Meat - minced
Acorn* mash
Egg yolk
Spring onion [optional]
Spices [optional]
Salt and pepper

Be brave son, worry not what the locals think when they see you gathering acorns. You are the one 'in the know'.

The first time the author rolled out this recipe minced pork was used in a 1:1 proportion with acorn flour and without any egg to bind the loaf. To be perfectly honest the texture of the 'fine' acorn flour didn't suit the recipe at all, though rougher acorn 'mash' really does complement the chopped meat texture. The choice of a wild game meat or something domesticated is down to you. This is also a good way of 'extending' your meat source in the outdoors.

Although the meat will 'set' when cooked the acorn component has no gluten content and weakens the 'loaf' so that it is quite fragile when turned out and hot. There are several options to deal with this... let the meatloaf cool down a little before turning out, add a tablespoon or two of flour, or add some egg yolk as mentioned. The latter is the author's preferred way, the egg adding richness to the final meatloaf as well as being a binder.

• Begin by squeezing as much water out of the acorn mash as possible. • Place the mash in a bowl and add the minced meat in a 1:1 proportion. • Add seasoning, and any other spices you wish [spring onions are excellent too]. • Then simply place the mixture in a very lightly oiled or greased baking tin or other container [it can even be a cereal dish]. • Cover the container top with foil, or by other means, and place in a pan containing some water - but not enough to engulf the meatloaf 'container' when at full boil.

• Cover the pan and bring to the boil, then keep at a gently rolling boil - topping up with more water as necessary. • Cooking time will vary from 30-60 minutes depending on the depth of meat in your container. • Once cooked, remove from the pan and allow to cool down - and firm up - for a few minutes, then slice into serving portions.

STUFFED DOCK LEAVES

Dock* leaves
Cup pre-cooked rice
2 cups ground meat
1 or 2 spring onions - finely chopped
Handful finely chopped leaves of choice
Salt, pepper, cinnamon
Butter or oil
2 cups water
½ cup lemon juice

Who needs to come down from the hills for a trip to the local Greek taverna when you have this recipe, which is an attempt at using our native wild plants to create a Greek dolmades equivalent?

• Wash the dock leaves [choose youngish ones where the central vein is not too large and tough, and remove the stems] then gently boil for several minutes in two changes of water to remove the bitterness. Drain. • Add chopped vegetables, seasoning, and melted butter or oil to the ground meat in a bowl. • Mix. If you still have any of the water left from cooking the rice, add a slug.

• Now put the leaves on a cutting board, the veined underside facing you. • Place a small amount of the meat mixture on the leaf and fold the stem end over it. • Then fold over the sides of the leaf [ie. tucking them in] and start to roll. You'll get the hang of it after a while.

• Put your rolled leaves in the bottom of a pan [lined with extra dock leaves to prevent sticking]. • Pour over the 2 cups of water and the lemon juice - though an alternative might be the acid-tasting qualities of common and sheep's sorrel chopped very finely and steeped in an equivalent amount of water. • Cover the pot and cook until tender.

VARIATIONS
Another alternative would be to use burdock leaves which have been gently boiled a couple of times to remove the bitterness.

GAME HUNTER'S CASSEROLE

Assorted game meats
Butter
2 or 3 large potatoes
2-3 medium onions - sliced
Water
Salt and pepper

This is such a simple, almost effortless, way of cooking a meal. • Cut whatever game you are using into portions that are roughly chop-sized then fry these until nicely browned all over. • Remove from pan and add some water to the pan to make a gravy stock. • Slice the onions. • Peel the potatoes, cutting in half if they are very large. • Place everything in a casserole dish then pour the gravy over and add some seasoning. • Cover, put in the oven at a moderate heat, and come back in 1½-2 hours time.

VARIATIONS

Why not try other starchy wild rootstocks as a potato substitute? Bullrush and reed tubers, wild angelica* or arrowhead roots for example.

VEGETABLE & MEAT SAUCE

½ cup red lentils
Butter or oil
2 cups diced meat
1 onion
Salt, pepper & cinnamon
1 cup each of chopped spring onions, leeks and good king henry
Nutmeg
2 cups water
1 tbsp. lemon juice [or sheep's sorrel-infused water]

• Start by cooking the split peas or lentils in water. • Season the meat and then sauté in butter or oil along with the chopped onion, until nicely browned. • In a second pan fry the chopped spring onion, leeks and good king henry [or substitute spinach] with a pinch of nutmeg.

• To the meat add the lemon juice and 2 cups of water, cover, and simmer for about 10-15 minutes or until the meat is tender. • Add the greens and red lentils to this about 15 minutes before serving. Serve with rice or couscous.

WATERCRESS BUBBLE and SQUEAK

Mashed potatoes
Watercress*
Leftover cooked meat
Butter or oil
Salt and pepper

True bubble and squeak uses cooked cabbage and many people like the savoury taste of corned beef as the meat source. This unusual version calls for the peppery leaves of watercress. However, because of the potential hazards with wild watercress it should be boiled or steamed first [*refer to note in Wild Plant Reference section*].

• Cook and mash the potatoes, add the cooked watercress, then add seasoning.
• Cut your meat leftovers into small pieces. • In a frying pan melt some butter [oil is a less salty alternative] and spoon in the mash and watercress mixture evenly in the pan. • Spread the diced meat over this, stir in and fry. The aim is to get the mixture on the pan bottom a nice golden brown, so only turn the mixture over occasionally.

VARIATIONS
Why not try the leaves of other wild plants as a replacement for the watercress, or cabbage in the traditional B&S? Good King Henry, nettles and suitably prepared ground-elder leaves would all make potential candidates. And why restrict the meat content when interesting taste combinations could be achieved with duck or pigeon, or even freshwater fish when used in a similar way?

ACORN & POTATO CAKES WITH BACON

1 cup acorn* mash	Spring onions
1 cup boiled potato	Bacon rashers
1 cup flour	Butter or oil
1 cup water	Salt [or not]

• Start by dicing the bacon. • Mix the acorn mash with the potatoes - which must also be mashed - then mix in the flour. • Add in a cupful of water - a bit at a time - and some spring onions chopped. Make sure the mash isn't too moist.

• From the combined 'mash' create some round patties and press these into your diced bacon. • Fry the patties in very hot oil until browned on both sides.

VARIATIONS
Depending on the saltiness of your bacon you may want to season accordingly.

In the absence of flour you can still make acorn-potato cakes. Just make sure that the potato mash is slightly dry which will help absorb some of the moisture in the acorn mash. Make the patties thinner - about potato cake thickness - and only fry in the minimum of oil. To add interest, add a hint of chilli powder and ground cinnamon when mixing the mash.

CHESTNUT & CORNED-BEEF BURGERS

Tinned corned beef
Chestnut meal / mash
Pepper or spices [optional]

Health-conscious readers will probably turn pale at the mention of corned beef, however a tin of ol' bully-beef is sometimes carried in the odd rucksack, so here's a simple way of doing something different with it. This recipe is also a good way of 'extending' corned beef.

• Working with a 1:1 proportion of the main ingredients, slice and roughly mash the corned beef. • Add to some prepared chestnut meal [see *Wild Plant Reference section* for preparation], and add pepper and spices if you wish. • Mix together thoroughly. • Form into small hamburger thickness patties about 3 inches wide. • Then fry in a very small amount of oil. • When turning make sure to support your burgers as they will be fragile.

VARIATIONS
For a really rich alternative combine an egg yolk with the mixture and some finely chopped spring onion. If you wish to increase the proportion of chestnut meal make sure to add some egg yolk for binding.

RABBIT REMPAH

2 cups rabbit meat - finely chopped / minced
1 cup grated / dessicated coconut
1 cup boiling water
1 garlic clove
Ground coriander and cumin seed
1 egg
Flour
Butter or oil
Salt

The author was wondering quite how to describe this Indonesian-style recipe but eventually left it at rempah - which is essentially a sort of mini meat burger. The recipe also calls for coconut which you won't find in the wilds unless you happen to carry some with you....

• Put the coconut meat in a bowl and add boiling water and allow to soak for 5-10 minutes. • Meanwhile, crush and paste the garlic clove, and beat the egg.

• Drain the water off the coconut and mix the moistened flakes with the minced rabbit in a bowl. • Add good pinches of the spices, the garlic, and a pinch of salt. • Mix everything together and dribble in some beaten egg and continue mixing - but don't make the mixture too moist. • Take heaped dessert spoonfuls of the mixture, roll into a ball and then slightly flatten – as if you were making falafel. • Dunk in some flour then fry in butter or oil for several minutes on each side and until cooked through.

WILDERNESS CAWL

Butter or oil
Onions
Parsnips or caraway / sweet cicely roots
Carrots [optional]
Swede [optional]
2 cups equivalent of meat
2-3 cups equivalent of bacon joint
Peppercorns
Stock [preferably a meat like lamb], or water
Potatoes or arrowhead tubers
Salt [if using water]

Traditional cawl is a Welsh one-pot dish with new ingredients added and being re-heated. There are many variations of cawl and the broth is often eaten separately from the other ingredients. Usually winter roots and beef or lamb are used but this version is one for outdoors people with fewer choices over precise ingredients. The meat content should be about 1 cup equivalent per person.

The 'optional' ingredients are those which you would expect to find in the traditional dish but you may not have access to these. For the meat content you might substitute rabbit portions or some game fowl.

• Roughly chop or slice all the vegetables - with the exception of the potatoes - and brown in butter or oil in a large pan. • Carefully remove from the oil and set aside. • Add the meat to the oil in the pan and brown all over. • Put the vegetables back in the pan and add the bacon [previously soaked if very salty], a good pinch of whole peppercorns, and the herbs [see variations note below].

• Cover the ingredients with stock or water, turn up the heat and bring to the boil. • Skim off the scum which develops after a couple of minutes, then turn down the heat to an oh-so-slow gentle simmer. • Simmer for 2-3 hours. • Thickly slice the potatoes and add in the last 20 minutes of cooking. • Serve [the meat sliced or portioned, along with some broth and vegetables].

VARIATIONS
A more traditional cawl might also include bay leaves, cloves and some fresh thyme, and would also have finely chopped raw leeks to garnish the dish.

GAME MARINADE

1 onion or 2-3 shallots
1 tbsp. olive oil
3 cups red wine
½ cup vinegar

3 or 4 bay leaves
Juniper* berries
Salt
Peppercorns

This is a very basic marinade that can be used for all sorts of game. However, it does rather hinge on getting some red wine... and it's only 5 miles to the offy.

• Begin by gently frying the onions in a stainless steel pan. • Once they have begun to brown add the red wine, vinegar, bay leaves, juniper berries and peppercorns. • Bring to the boil then simmer very gently for about 15 minutes. During this taste a little of the liquor and season.

VENISON STEW

3 cups venison - cubed	1 can tomatoes
Flour	2 cups red wine
Salt and pepper	1½ cups water
Thyme and oregano	1 garlic clove
2 onions	Potatoes
Butter or oil	Vegetables - sliced

• Dunk the meat cubes in seasoned flour laced with thyme and oregano. • In a large pan brown the onions in butter or oil. • Remove onions from pan and set aside. • Similarly sauté the meat, ensuring that the cubes are sealed all round by the heat.

• Put the onions back in the pan with the meat and add the can of tomatoes, wine and water, and a whole clove of garlic. • Cover and simmer for about 30-40 minutes. • Then add sliced vegetables - potatoes, celery and carrots, or wild food alternatives. • Simmer gently for about another 30 minutes or until the vegetables are tender.

VENISON & ACORN STEW

Venison
Onions
Acorn* mash
Water
Chilli [optional]
Salt and pepper

• Cube the venison and slice the onions and gently sauté in a pan until they start to brown. • Add seasoning and water to cover. • Simmer slowly for an hour or until the meat is tender. • Remove meat and stir in 1 to 2 cups of acorn mash to the liquid, bring to the boil then simmer for a few minutes [reduce as required]. • Dish the venison and pour the broth over.

VENISON STROGANOFF

2 cups venison - sliced	Paprika
1 onion	Cream
1 or 2 garlic cloves	Sherry [optional]
Mushrooms	Salt and pepper
Butter	

• Cut the venison into thin diagonal slivers. • Season lightly with salt and pepper. • Heat some butter in a heavy pan at a high heat and sauté the meat until lightly browned. You may need to do this in batches. • Remove meat from pan and set aside.

• The onions should be halved lengthwise and then sautéd in butter along with the crushed garlic, and thickly sliced mushrooms. • Stir often until the onions are lightly browned. • Reduce the heat, add a good sprinkle of paprika and the cream, and stir at a medium heat for about 5 minutes, making sure that the cream does not curdle. Add a slug of sherry if you like.

• Combine the cooked meat with the sauce and simmer gently for another 10-15 minutes. Serve with rice.

VENISON THAI CURRY & HAZELNUT SAUCE

2 cups venison - sliced
1-3 tsp. Thai red curry paste
2 cups coconut cream
1-2 tbsp. sugar [or honey]
Lemon juice
½ cup ground hazelnuts
Salt and pepper

If one were being true to Thai cuisine then this recipe would include traditional ingredients like lemon grass, fish sauce and palm sugar... and yes the Thai curry paste is best! Not exactly what you expect to find when out on the hills, agreed. So inevitably this recipe takes shortcuts but provides an interesting variation on serving up venison. Ingredient proportions can be shifted depending on your preferred heat, sweetness and texture levels.

• Slice the venison into strips about 3 inches long and about ¼-inch thick. • Very lightly fry the venison till it just firms up. • Remove from the heat and allow the meat to 'relax'.

• Meanwhile put the coconut cream in a thick bottomed pan or casserole - keeping a little back to mix the curry paste with later. [If using dried coconut cream make up 2 cups equivalent with boiling water.] • Bring the coconut cream to the boil, stirring to stop it sticking. • Add curry paste to taste and cook for several minutes before adding some sugar and a good twist of lemon juice. • Simmer for a few minutes then bring to a gentle boil. • Add the venison and ground hazelnuts [these replace peanuts that you would expect in true Thai cooking.] • Cook for about another 10 minutes adding some seasoning. Serve.

VENISON MEAT LOAF

2 or 3 cups venison - minced	Juniper* berries
1 onion	Port [optional]
1 garlic clove [optional]	Salt and pepper
Butter or oil	Breadcrumbs or oat meal
2 eggs	

• Slice the onion and garlic and sauté until slightly brown. • Add to venison mince in a bowl, along with the eggs, seasoning, a few juniper berries, a splash of port and fold everything together. • Grease a baking tin, sprinkle the breadcrumbs or oatmeal around the inside, then fill the baking tin with the meat [an alternative is to form the meat into a roll and wrap with bacon]. • Cover lightly with foil and bake in a moderate oven for about an hour.

FRIED VENISON WITH BROOM PICKLES

Venison - thinly sliced
Butter and oil
Lemon juice
Broom* pickles - or capers
Wild salad leaves
Salt and pepper

If they were good enough for Henry VIII – broom pickles that is – then surely they are good enough for you.

• Season the thinly sliced meat, then fry for a few minutes until cooked. • In a bowl mix your wild salad leaves - chopped if necessary - with a handful of broom pickles. [see page 179] • Drizzle over some oil and lemon juice. • Add the fried venison and toss the contents of the bowl. Serve.

ALTERNATIVES
If you are unable to get lemon juice a good flavoured vinegar would do. You could also use the RASPBERRY VINAIGRETTE recipe as another alternative.

GAME LIVER RAVIOLI

Bacon
Liver – venison, rabbit or game fowl
Small onion
Salt and pepper
Butter or oil

'Ere mate, lend us your gondola...

This recipe comes in two parts – the pasta and the stuffing. First make some authentic pasta [see recipe for HOMEMADE PASTA] for cutting into ravioli type pasta envelopes.

As for the stuffing that is made with the liver of any game that you were recently cooking up and were wondering what to do with those odd leftover inside bits.

• Begin by chopping the liver as fine as you can. • Then finely chop and then sauté a small onion until soft. • Remove from the pan and fry the bacon. • Remove this from the pan and chop the bacon finely, then set aside. • Put the chopped liver into the frying pan and cook until it is done – but with a little pinkness. • Turn the cooked liver into a bowl along with the onion and fried bacon.

• The next job is to mash the ingredients together to produce a coarse purée [a blender would be ideal but is rather impractical in the field], and add seasoning. • Place small dollops of this mixture on your ravioli squares, dampen the edges of the pasta with beaten egg then fold over and seal. • Allow the ravioli to dry out for about 30 minutes, turning over once midway. • Drop the pasta into salted boiling water, then reduce the heat and simmer gently for about 10 minutes. • Extract, drain and serve with a sauce.

CHESTNUT TAGLIATELLI & BACON

½ cup flour
½ cup chestnut meal or flour
1 egg
1 tsp. oil

Bacon
Mushrooms
Butter or oil
Cream

Explore the *WILD* side of pasta with this offering. The savoury bacon and mushroom sauce complements the slight sweetness of the pasta quite well, but it could equally be a cheese or tomato-based sauce.

• Begin by mixing the flour and chestnut in a bowl. If using mashed chestnuts make sure they are as dry as possible – if necessary alter the proportion of flour to compensate for moisture in the chestnuts. • Add the egg to the bowl and the oil and mix until a ball of dough forms. • Take dough from the bowl and knead. • Allow to dough rest for half an hour [if you're hungry don't bother with that].

• Dust a flat surface with some flour and roll the pasta thinly. • Dust the top of the pasta and gently roll up. • Using a sharp knife cut across the roll to form the tagliatelli strips - no more than about ¼-inch in width. • Unravel and spread strips on a flour dusted flat surface or hang somewhere to dry for about an hour.

• Meanwhile, slice the mushrooms. • Remove fat from bacon and dice the meat. • Gently fry the bacon in a very little oil then remove from the pan. • Lightly fry the mushrooms till they soften. • Stir in some cream and heat gently. • Return the bacon back to the pan and stir in.

• Drop your tagliatelli into some boiling water and cook for about 3-5 minutes or until tender. • Drain, and drop the tagliatelli into the sauce. • Heat through gently for a few minutes, then serve.

ALTERNATIVES
An acorn pasta dough made in a proportion of 75% acorn flour / 25% flour [3:1] is also excellent. Try a pepper, or tomato and mushroom sauce to accompany.

VENISON & BARLEY SOUP

2-3 cups cooked, diced venison
2-3 pints venison [or beef] stock
2 cups barley
1-2 onions

This is a simple soup which can make use of meat leftovers. • Slice the onions and combine with the rest of the ingredients in a large pan. • Bring to the boil, cover and then simmer for about 40-45 minutes or until the barley has cooked.

VARIATIONS
The more barley you add the thicker the soup will be. Obviously other meats can replace the venison, and you may also like to add some greens - the celery-like stalks of alexanders, for example, or ½ a cup of lovage*, or several handfuls of wild vegetable greens, but do not use sorrel as it will turn to sludge with the long cooking time. A handful of burdock root will add something crunchy too.

BACON, SWEET CICELY & GREENS SOUP

Bacon joint
Sweet cicely roots
Wild greens
Pepper

This recipe is really an opportunity to deal with a 'real' salted bacon joint in a less traditional way.

• Soak the bacon joint for several hours to extract most of the salt, then put the joint in a large pan and add fresh water. • Bring to the boil for several minutes and then reduce the heat to a rapid simmer and cook until done. Skim off any scum that forms on the water surface.

• Add chopped sweet cicely roots, wild greens and season with pepper. The choice of roughly chopped greens will depend on what is available to you. Perhaps shepherd's purse for a more cabbage-like flavour. • Continue to cook until the leaves and roots are tender, then serve the soup with the bacon sliced or chopped.

VARIATIONS
Sweet cicely roots could be substituted by other wild rootstocks like arrowhead or meadow goat's beard.

SQUIRREL

A friend who has tried squirrel says that it is tough, and researching about squirrel on the Net revealed one American food writer suggesting that squirrel is best s-l-o-w cooked at a very low heat for up to 8 hours. Other Net-based recipes offer all sort of ways of baking, roasting and stewing the meat.

FEATHERY THINGS

PIGEON TIKKA MASALA

Pigeon meat
2-3 garlic cloves
1 medium onion
Oil
Water [Chicken stock preferred]
Chilli powder – pinch

1 tsp each of ground coriander, cumin
and paprika
1-2 tbsp. lemon juice
Plain yoghurt - 1 carton
Salt

The Guild of Master Curry Stirrers will no doubt rebel, though there's probably some soul in a distant corner of the world tucking into this right now.

For many years Chicken Tikka – CTM to its die-hard friends - was the Brits' favourite dish, so how about using some imagination and extending it to pigeon, or perhaps even rabbit which may be more akin to chicken meat?

• Create the marinade by mixing together the spice ingredients, lemon juice [lime if you can get it], yoghurt and a pinch of salt. • Place the pigeon meat in the marinade and make sure that every piece gets a covering. Ideally the meat should marinade for 24-hours in a fridge or cool place [remember we are dealing with game fowl here], but if you are on the move an hour is better than nothing at all.

• In a frying pan heat the oil till it is very hot, then add the meat. • Stir-fry for a several minutes. • Set the pieces aside and keep warm. • Finely chop the onion and garlic [ramsons will do too, but they will lose most of their garlic properties] and fry until they start to brown. • Add the pigeon meat back to the frying pan, along with any marinade left over and water [chicken stock would be much better]. • Simmer until the meat is cooked and the sauce thickened. Serve.

NETTLES & CHESTNUT STUFFED PIGEON

2 pigeons
Chestnuts
1 onion
Butter or oil
Ramsons leaf [optional]
2 pints of water
1-2 pints nettles
Handful of fat-hen seed [oat or barley meal can substitute]
Salt and pepper

• Begin by boiling the chestnuts - which will be used for stuffing the pigeon - until tender. Then mash coarsely. • Chop the onion finely and fry till it softens. • Add the chestnuts to the pan and cook for a few minutes more, adding a bit of seasoning. • Add too, the garlicky ramsons leaf chopped if you want. • Take off the heat and then stuff the pigeon with this mixture.

• Truss or skewer the bird to seal in the stuffing, place in a pan, add the water and bring to the boil. • Cover and simmer for about 30-35 minutes. • Then add a sufficient quantity of nettles as the vegetable ingredient plus the fat-hen seeds to the liquor, stir in, and cook for another 10 minutes. Serve.

VARIATIONS
You may like to add the pigeon's liver to the stuffing mixture, but best fry first.

PIGEON WITH GINGER & COCONUT

Pigeon meat
Ginger – root preferred
Lemon juice
Butter and oil
Coconut cream
Stock - optional
Salt and pepper

• Remove meat from the bone and use the carcass to make some stock [for possible use in this recipe or for a separate dish].

• Grate some ginger root [powdered ginger will do but it is really not as good for this dish], and mix with several large slugs of lemon juice in a bowl along with some oil. • Add the pigeon pieces to the bowl and mix thoroughly so that all pieces get coated. • Allow to marinate for at least 30 minutes then drain off, but keep, whatever is left of the marinade.

• Heat some butter or oil in a frying pan and sauté the pigeon pieces until they are lightly browned. • Remove meat from the pan and keep warm.

The next steps of the recipe vary depending on what source of coconut you have available....

• Add whatever is left of the marinade to the pan [if you prefer a less 'hot' dish strain out the grated ginger], then add the coconut ingredient. [If you have canned coconut milk simply add to the pan. If you are using a block of coconut cream then crumble it into some pigeon stock - yes, the one mentioned at the start of the recipe - then add to the pan.] • Continue cooking until a nice rich sauce develops which coats the back of a spoon. • Add pigeon meat and gently simmer for 10-12 minutes. • Drizzle the sauce over the served pigeon meat. • Best served with rice, but could liven up other wild rootstocks.

PIGEON WITH CHESTNUTS

1 pigeon per person - minimum
1 pint water
Chestnuts - peeled
Soy sauce
Oil
Spring onion
1 tbsp. cornflour

A recipe with a slight Chinese accent. • Halve the pigeons, place in a pan with a pint of water and oh-so-slowly gently simmer for about 30-40 minutes. • Add the oil, several good slugs of soy sauce and the chestnuts and cook for another ½ hour on a low heat. • Mix a little cornflour with some of the cooking liquid into a paste and then add to the pan and cook till it thickens. • Halve a whole spring onion and then slice lengthways and add to the pan. Cook for a few minutes more.

PIGEON WITH RICE

2-3 cups diced pigeon meat
Butter or oil
Large onion
2-3 cups rice
Salt
Pepper
Cinnamon
Cup of dried elderberries

• Cook the rice so that it absorbs the cooking water but is not quite cooked through. • Finely chop the onion and fry in the butter or oil until the pieces are golden brown. • Remove, and set aside. • Similarly sauté the pigeon along with pinches of salt, pepper and cinnamon. • Take the washed elderberries and very gently warm in oil or butter over a low heat.

Now you need to combine the ingredients in a baking dish... • Take some oil or melted better and coat the bottom of the dish before spreading the rice evenly on the bottom. • On top of this distribute the other ingredients you have been preparing. • Drizzle with a little more oil or melted butter, cover with foil and place in a medium-hot oven for 10-15 minutes, before reducing to a low heat and cooking for another 30-40 minutes. What you should end up with is crispy golden rice on the bottom and fluffy white rice above.

SPICY PLUM PIGEONS

Pigeons - minimum one each
Butter and oil
Flour
Onion
Cloves and cinnamon
Plums - about 2-3 per person
Red wine

Humble birds, born without the slightest hint of plummyness in their mouths...

• Finely chop an onion and coat the pigeons lightly in flour. • Sauté the onions until they are soft and set aside. • In the same pan fry the pigeons until they are gently browned all over, then put in a casserole or oven dish. • Add the onions and pinches of cinnamon and cloves - or grated herb bennett root to replace the clove spice.

• Add about a cup of red wine to the frying pan, bring to the boil and stir to absorb all the flavours. • Pour the liquor over the pigeons, and arrange the plums around. • Cover well with foil or use the lid and bake in a pre-heated moderate oven for about 1-1½ hours or until the pigeons are done. • Thicken the juices if necessary before serving.

HONEY GLAZED PIGEON ROAST

Pigeons - 1 per person minimum
Salt and pepper
Celery or wild substitute
Onions
Sage - fresh preferably
Clear honey

Here 'roasting' is a bit of a misnomer since you may want to tackle the cooking of this in two ways, depending on your circumstances - either in a roasting pan in a preheated medium oven, or foil wrapped and placed over embers and essentially braising the pigeon.

• Season the pigeons inside and out. • Create a stuffing of diced celery [or a wild alternative], chopped onion, and fresh sage - if you can get it. • Stuff the birds and truss. • Place on your roasting dish or foil and brush with honey [maple syrup would be a tasty replacement]. Cover with foil when roasting. • If using an oven, roast until the juices run clear when the meat is pricked, but baste the birds with the honey-rich juices from time to time. • If following the foil method, cook until the meat separates easily from the bone.

PICKLED PIGEON

2 pigeons
1 tbsp. salt
1 tbsp. sugar
1 tsp. saltpetre
3 pints chicken stock
3 pints cold water

One to try if you have time on your hands and want to explore something more unusual than pickled onions and gherkins – and no, the pigeon doesn't explode!

• Mix the saltpetre, sugar and salt together and then rub this onto the birds, making sure the inside is coated too. • Place in a small bowl or vessel and pour the cold water over. • Leave to absorb the mixture for 12 hours in a cool place.

• To cook, rinse off the mixture, put the pigeon in a pan with the chicken stock and bring to the boil. • Reduce the heat to a barely active simmer and cook for about 45 minutes to an hour, or until the bird's leg is almost tender enough to come away with little effort. Serve.

PIGEON WALDORF SALAD

Pigeon - cooked
Celery stalks or wild alternative [burdock]
Eating apple
Dates
Hazelnuts or beech masts
Mayonnaise
Lemon juice
Salt and pepper

Mimicking that world famous salad this version calls for one or two ingredients beyond the camper's expected larder. But then.... be inspired.

• Dice the cooked pigeon meat. • Chop the celery cross-wise into ¼-inch pieces, dice the apple and dates, and the hazelnuts roughly. Beech masts can be left whole. • Place these ingredients in a bowl and add mayonnaise, a splash of lemon juice and some seasoning. • Mix well together. Enjoy.

VARIATIONS
You could try replacing the celery with the blanched and refreshed young stems of alexanders.

CRAB-APPLE & PIGEON SAUCE

1 smallish onion
Butter or oil
Lemon juice
2 cups of diced pigeon
Butter or oil
Salt
Water
3-4 handfuls of crab-apples

• Gently fry the finely chopped onion till golden brown, then remove from the heat and add a slug of lemon juice. • Separately sauté the pigeon meat until browned and season as required, before adding a good splash of water and a slug of lemon juice. • Turn the heat down and simmer until the meat is tender.

• Meanwhile take the crab-apples and split in half and remove as much of the core as possible. • Then slice each half into 2 or 3 slices, and sauté in butter for about 5-8 minutes. • Combine the onions with the meat and top with the apple pieces. • Simmer gently for a further 5-10 minutes. Serve with rice or potatoes.

VARIATIONS
Normally pork is associated with apple, but since crab-apples can be very tart it seemed that a more gamey flesh might be appropriate, hence the pigeon. Rabbit is possibly too mild in flavour. Try with duck.

PIGEON, HAM & HAZLENUT STEW

Gammon ham	1 pint beer or Guinness
Butter or oil	Water
Pigeons	Bay leaves
Mushrooms	Salt and pepper
Hazlenuts	

• Cut the gammon ham into several large chunks then fry in oil in a heavy pan until sealed and slightly browned. • Add the pigeons and brown as much of the outside as possible. • Tip in the mushrooms [halved if large], and a good handful of roughly halved hazelnuts. • Stir and continue to cook until the mushrooms begin to soften. • Add the beer or Guinness, a slug of water, couple of bay leaves and seasoning.

• Bring to a boil for a few minutes, then cover and simmer gently for about an hour, or until the meat on the pigeons easily separates from the bone. • Remove from the heat, take out the gammon pieces and pigeon, and set aside. • Skim off any large excess of fat from the liquor in the pan then reduce the liquid further and pour over the served meat.

PIGEON OR PHEASANT BROTH

Pigeon or pheasant
Bacon or ham
Alexanders, sweet cicely, lovage* or burdock stem
2 large onions
Butter or oil
2 pints water
Peppercorns
Bread

A recipe to use up the leftovers of game fowl or older birds. If you decide to use lovage* only use about ½ cup of the chopped stalk, otherwise use 1 cup of the other alternatives.

• Dice the meat, chop the stick of a wild celery-like equivalent [but beware lovage] reasonably finely, slice the onions lengthwise, plus 2 or 3 sliced rashers of bacon or 1 slice of chopped gammon ham. • Fry the ingredients until they are slightly browned. • Remove and place in a pan, adding the water and a few peppercorns. • Bring to the boil, then reduce the heat and simmer for about 30 minutes. • Meanwhile, cube the bread and fry in some oil or butter and serve up with the broth, or use a wild thickener.

VARIATIONS
To add thickness and more substance to the broth you may like to add pearl barley or groats.

DUCK & PIGEON MEAT LOAF

2 cups diced duck	1 cup milk or water
2 cups diced pigeon	1 onion - grated
1 egg	Salt and pepper
½ cup flour	Breadcrumbs [optional]

• Mix the egg with the meat in a bowl, then gradually work in the flour and milk. • Finally add the grated onion and seasoning. • Grease a suitable bread mould or baking tin, and if you want to use the breadcrumb option sprinkle these around now. • Fill the tin with your meat mixture and level off.

• Place the mould into a baking tray or other similar flat dish able to hold water, and half fill this with water. • Put in a moderately hot oven and cook for about an hour. • To serve, flip the mould over onto a dish and slice portions of your meat loaf. Perhaps serve with a nice fruity country sauce.

NUT STUFFED DUCK

Duck breast
Beech masts [or hazelnuts]
Stilton cheese
Orange juice
Salt and pepper

The idea behind this recipe was to create a very rich filling which takes little time to prepare. It uses some very pungent ingredients and you may find that one portion is ample for two.

• Crush the masts with the flat blade of a kitchen knife and moisten with a little orange or lemon juice.

• Keeping the skin on the duck breast place the meat skin side down on a chopping board and beat quite thin with a steak hammer. • Spread the crushed masts on the meat and dot with several small slivers of stilton cheese. • Roll up the meat and secure with some natural fibre string. • Place on kitchen foil and close the foil around, place on an oven tray and cook in a pre-heated moderate to moderately-hot oven for about 20 minutes. • Drizzle the cooking juices over the meat when serving.

VARIATIONS
Honey or port could be used to moisten the masts and so provide a sweeter alternative.

DUCK WITH ELDERBERRIES

Duck Meat
Butter or oil
Salt and pepper
Elderberries - ripe
Chestnuts
Milk

• Cut the duck into strips and fry gently. • Once cooked, remove from the heat and season.

• Put most of the elderberries into a saucepan with a knob of butter and heat slowly, pressing the berries with a spoon to release the juice. • Strain off the flesh of the fruit and then raise the heat to reduce the liquid. What you are looking for with the sauce is a thick consistency which coats the duck pieces rather than swims around the plate. • Add the fried duck pieces to the sauce and heat for a few minutes more. • Serve with the remainder of the uncooked berries as a garnish.

VARIATIONS

To 'warm' the flavour of the elderberry sauce why not consider trying the addition of cinnamon, cloves or nutmeg? Pigeon meat might be a replacement for duck, and venison might be worth a try. As a replacement to the elderberries try a glazing sauce of honey, brown sugar and Guinness along with nutmeg and cinnamon spices.

DUCK WITH WILD CHERRIES

1 duck	1 cup water
1 small onion	1-2 cups cherries
1 garlic clove	Sugar
Marjoram and basil	Salt and pepper
Red wine	

• First, rub the duck inside and out with salt then place in a casserole dish with the onion sliced in half. • Crush the garlic and smear over the duck, then daub the bird with the herbs.

• Pour the water and wine into the casserole, add some seasoning, cover and then cook in a moderate oven until the duck is tender - about 1-1½ hours depending on size.

• Remove the duck from the casserole and strain the juices into a pan. • Heat the liquid until boiling and then add the stoned cherries, stir until they a very soft, and add sugar to taste. • Simmer until the liquid forms a nice thick sauce, and serve up with the duck.

SPICY DUCK COUSCOUS

Couscous	Cinnamon
Duck meat - sliced	Butter or oil
Paprika or cayenne	Dried fruit [optional]
Hazelnuts or beech masts	Salt

Couscous is such a simple staple to prepare - taking only a few minutes - that it is something you should consider carrying on outdoors trips. It is also very much a middle-eastern item, hence this spicy interpretation. If you can get some dried dates and raisins this will give your dish a more authentic feel.

• Begin by placing the dry couscous in a bowl and pouring some boiling water [or stock] over and leaving the grains to absorb.

• Put a little oil in a pan, heat and add a good pinch of paprika [cayenne if you like things hotter]. • Sauté the duck pieces until brown then set aside.

• Roughly chop the hazelnuts and sauté in a little oil or butter along with a pinch of ground cinnamon powder. When the nuts just begin to brown remove from the heat. • Fluff up the couscous and combine the hazelnuts. Serve with the sliced duck laid on top.

FAT-HEN, DUCK & ORANGE SAUCE

2 cups finely chopped duck meat   1 cup water
2 small onions   ½ cup orange juice
Butter or oil   1 tbsp. lemon juice
Salt and pepper   ½ tbsp. flour
1 pint fresh fat-hen leaves

• Mix the duck meat, finely chopped onion and seasoning, then form into small meatballs before frying for 10 minutes until nicely browned.

• Chop the fat-hen leaves and gently wilt in butter in a second pan for about 10 minutes. • Combine the vegetables with the duck and add a cup of water. • Simmer gently for about 15 minutes.

• Mix orange and lemon juice with the flour, then add this to the meat and vegetables, seasoning if necessary. • Simmer for a further 20 minutes.

VARIATIONS
Try beef instead of duck, and incorporating some finely chopped leaves of ramsons - or hedge garlic - into the meatballs.

BILBERRY & SPICY PHEASANT

Pheasant breasts
Pinches of paprika, cumin, mustard powder, cayenne, black pepper
Butter or oil
1 onion
½ cup red wine
1-2 cups bilberries
Salt

• Finely chop the onion. • Mix good pinches of the spices together and sprinkle over both sides of the pheasant breasts.

• Place some oil in a pan and sauté the meat until it is cooked through [or slightly pink if you like it like that], then remove from the pan but keep warmed. • Add the chopped onion to the pan and soften, then add the red wine, stirring well. • Cook until the liquid is much reduced and add the bilberries. • Simmer gently for 5-10 minutes. • Season to taste and pour over the pheasant breasts.

HONEY & HAZELNUT ROAST PHEASANT

½-¾ cup clear honey
Cider vinegar - slug
Hazelnuts - chopped
Soy sauce [optional]
1 pheasant

• Combine the honey, vinegar and chopped hazelnuts and gently simmer. Splash a bit of soy sauce into this mixture too if you wish.

• Drizzle the sauce over your prepared pheasant, cover with foil and then place in a preheated moderate oven and roast for 1-1½ hours depending on size, basting from time to time with the honey mixture in the bottom of the roasting dish.

ALTERNATIVES
A completely different alternative you might like to try is stuffing your pheasant with lentils and chopped bacon or ham. Also consider serving pheasant with a creamy onion sauce.

PHEASANT & SPICY HAZELNUT SAUCE

Pheasant
1 onion
Tomato purée [optional]
1-1½ cups hazelnuts
1 garlic clove

Chilli powder and turmeric
Salt
Lemon juice
Oil
½ pint water

• Skin, bone and cube the pheasant meat. • Chop the hazelnuts reasonably finely. • Pulp the garlic clove. • Chop the onion finely and then mash to the best of your ability - for readers with a blender, use that, or your personal assistant. • Turn into a bowl and add a squidge of tomato paste, the nuts, good pinches of the spices and salt, the garlic and a good slug of lemon juice. • Mix together very well [perform this stage in the blender for a really smooth sauce].

• Heat some oil in a pan [large enough to hold all the meat] at about medium heat - and add the sauce mixture. • Fry for a few minutes, keeping the sauce stirred to prevent sticking, and reducing the heat if necessary to prevent burning.

• Add the pheasant meat and continue frying for a couple more minutes.
• Then add the water, alter the temperature to a low simmering point, cover, and cook for another 10-15 minutes or until the meat is cooked through and sauce has thickened. Best served with rice.

VARIATIONS

For a slightly more authentic Indian sauce add a bit of yoghurt when combining all the sauce ingredients together, and you could add some sultanas or other dried fruit to complement the spicy flavour.

BAKED FRUITED PHEASANT

Pheasant
Ginger
Salt
Barberries
Gooseberries
Butter

The inspiration for this comes from a mid-sixteenth century recipe - but much simplified for outdoors cooking. It could be adapted to duck or pigeon and other fruits could be used.

• If you have access to real grated ginger root rather than ginger powder so much the better, but in any case rub salt and ginger over the bird. • Place on double thickness cooking foil large enough to enclose the bird. • Place barberries and gooseberries around the bird and some in the cavity. • Put several knobs of butter on the top of the bird and then draw up the foil and crimp the edges. • Bake until done - either in an oven, over embers, or in a hangi - probably about 2-3 hours cooking time in the latter case.

PHEASANT BAKE

Pheasant - jointed	Stalk vegetables
Flour or meal	Onions
Oil	Crab-apples
Potatoes	Salt and pepper

• Take the pheasant pieces and flour, and brown in a pan with some oil.
• Prepare the vegetables, cutting into pieces. Stem vegetables can include things like alexanders, lovage* leaf stalks, or even domesticated celery. • Lastly prepare the crab-apples. They should preferably be peeled, but must be halved and their cores removed. If you haven't the patience for small apples then sliced cooking apples are an alternative.

• Arrange all the vegetables and apples in a suitable oven dish then add enough water to just cover them. • Place the pheasant on top and add seasoning. • Cover, and bake in a moderate oven until cooked. • Some of the cooking juices can be thickened up for gravy.

PHEASANT-AU-VIN

Pheasant - jointed
Mushrooms
Small onions or shallots
Butter and oil [preferably olive]
Salt and pepper
Red wine
Flour
Cloves [herb bennett root] and cinnamon stick [optional]

Not an adventurous recipe to be sure, but an effortless way to cook a large bird or tackle those of dubious old buzzard-like age - assuming you can lay your hands on some wine in the outdoors.

• Gently fry the mushrooms [halve if very large] and halved shallots in butter till the onions start to brown. • Remove from the pan and set aside. • Add oil to the pan and gently fry the pheasant joints until slightly browned. • Remove and place in a casserole with the fried onions and mushrooms, and add seasoning.

• With the frying pan still on the heat add the best part of a bottle of wine and stir to absorb all the cooking juices. • Stir in several pinches of flour to thicken the liquid a little and cook for a couple of minutes longer. • Pour over the casserole contents. The use of a few cloves and a piece of cinnamon stick is optional - the latter will bring a warm spiciness to the dish. • Cover the casserole and place in a preheated moderate-ish oven for an hour or until done.

PHEASANT & CRAB-APPLES

Pheasant - portioned
Butter or oil
Crab-apples - or cookers
2-3 tsp. sugar
Salt and pepper
Cream
Breadcrumbs

• Sauté the pheasant pieces until browned all over then remove from the pan and set aside.

• Split the crab-apples, remove the core material and place them in the frying pan and cook over a gentle heat with the sugar till they begin to soften. Remove from the heat.

• Place the partly cooked apples in the bottom of an ovenproof dish or casserole, followed by the pheasant pieces and some seasoning. • Cover and cook in a pre-heated moderate oven for about 30-40 minutes. • Remove briefly from the oven and pour in some cream - to taste, but not more than about a cup. • Stir in among the apples and return to the oven for another 5-10 minutes [overall cooking time will depend on bird size/age, extending to 60 minutes for older birds]. • Meanwhile, fry the breadcrumbs in a little oil and sprinkle these over the dish when serving.

VARIATIONS
It is an unusual combination but in the absence of cream you could try experimenting with coconut cream as the dairy substitute, or simply go on a diet.

You could also use this method for a very basic and simple duck with orange dish, although there wouldn't be the need for pre-softening the orange pieces.

BRAISED SPICY PHEASANT

Pheasant
Lemon juice
Butter and oil
Tomatoes - purée and canned
Water
1 cup dry white wine
Cloves or herb bennett
Cinnamon
Salt and pepper

• Portion the pheasant, place in a bowl and squeeze over some lemon juice; using fingers to ensure all parts are coated. • Allow to marinade while you prepare some other ingredients... • Chop the canned tomatoes and also thin a good squidge of tomato purée with water or juice from the canned tomatoes.

• If using herb bennett root as a clove substitute, peel a portion of the root and then grate the stem finely - or peel and cut several segments to be removed before serving.

• Next, heat some oil or butter in a casserole or heavy based pan and sauté the pheasant pieces until nicely browned. • Pour in the wine and simmer. • Add the tomatoes and stir in the thinned purée, followed by several cloves or the herb bennett, a cinnamon stick or teaspoon of the ground spice, and seasoning. • Cover and reduce the heat to an oh-so-slow low simmer and cook for about an hour, or until the pheasant is tender. • Add a little more water [or even wine] during cooking if things appear to be becoming dry.

PHEASANT BBQ

Pheasant pieces
Oil
1 medium onion
1 garlic clove
1 tsp. each of paprika, chilli, black pepper, cayenne
1 tsp. salt
1 tbsp. sugar [or molasses]

Here's one for a barbie with a difference...

To prepare the BBQ sauce you really need a blender, mortar and pestle, or some way of pasting the onion and garlic clove. An alternative would be onion and garlic powder.

• To a little oil add all the spice ingredients, onion and garlic, and sugar to produce a paste which can be smeared onto your dried-off pheasant pieces.
• All that remains is to barbecue the meat.

VARIATIONS
Some off-the-shelf BBQ mixtures have a sweet and sour tomato flavour, while homemade BBQ sauces frequently include tomato ketchup. If you prefer that sort of taste then simply add some tomato paste and vinegar to the spice mixture above. Sauce can also be used with 'barbied' rabbit.

VEGETABLE & PHEASANT MEATBALLS

3 tbsp. yellow split peas / red lentils   Salt
2 tbsp. rice   Tomato purée
2-3 cups pheasant meat - minced   Butter or oil
1 small & 1 large onion   Pepper and cinnamon
Some orange peel - optional   Lemon juice
1 egg   1 ½ cups water

• Separately cook the split peas and rice till tender. • Meanwhile, chop the small onion finely and add to the meat, egg, orange peel and seasoning in a bowl. • Add the rice and split peas to the bowl and mix further, before forming the mixture into balls.

• Chop the larger of the onions finely and then fry in some melted butter or oil along with several large dollops of tomato purée. • Fry until the onion begins to brown. • Add 1 ½ cups of water and the juice of a lemon and simmer for about 10 minutes. • Gently add the meatballs to this, cover and simmer for another 30 minutes. • About half way through baste the meatballs, and if necessary add a little more water to keep the developing sauce liquid.

HONEY PHEASANT & MUSTARD SALAD

Pheasant
Mustard
Clear honey
Butter or oil
Mustard greens - young
Boiled potatoes or arrowhead tubers
Salt and pepper

• Place some clear honey in a bowl, add mustard powder or prepared mustard and mix together. • Drop in skinless pieces of pheasant meat and coat with the mixture. If there is time let the pieces marinate for a longer period.

• Remove excess honey mixture from the pheasant pieces and sauté until nicely browned on both sides and any juices run clear. • Take off the heat, remove meat from the pan and add a little water. • Place back on the heat and stir for another minute to absorb the flavours in the pan. • Dice the potatoes [preferably still warm] and mix with young salad mustard greens. • Drizzle the liquor in the pan over and toss. Serve with the pheasant pieces.

GAME FOWL 'OLIVES'

This is not so much of a recipe as some ideas to inspire you on preparing various game meat - duck and pigeon, to rabbit and venison - in a similar manner to beef olives... interpreting the meat and flavours with whatever comes to hand in the outdoors.

To explain [for the 'non-foodies' among readers]... In true 'beef olives' lean beef steak is beaten with a steak hammer until the meat it is about one quarter inch thick. After seasoning, and sometimes buttering, the meat is then wrapped round a stuffing mixture and tied in place with string [non-synthetic]. Some cooks will then lightly fry the olives to seal the meat before placing on an oven tray and baking uncovered in a moderate for about 30 minutes or until done [the timing very much depends on the thickness of the meat and stuffing]. That is the basic theory. Now to create your own alternatives, and some starting suggestions...

• For large game fowl use breast meat that is boneless and skinless. • Beat the meat flat - under a plastic bag or cling film will make the job easier - and make it slightly less than a quarter of an inch thick. • Lay the meat out on a flat surface, lightly oil or butter and then place you filling layer on top. • For a savoury 'pheasant olive' you might consider chopped hazelnuts and spices, for duck why not try something sweetish with a bit of lemon rind to add a tang? For pigeon - the breasts are tiny - how about something creamy?

The idea could even be extended to rabbit fillets, beaten thin and then covered with a slice of Swiss cheese followed by a slice of cooked ham. If using venison, why not try a really hot spicy flavour alongside some mashed sweet chestnuts as the main filling?

• When you've sorted the filling, roll up the meat like a Swiss roll - which is where these 'olives' differ from the traditional type. • Rather than using string - since you are in the great outdoors - fashion some natural cocktail sticks from small sharpened twigs and push them through the rolls to keep the meat together. • Finally, it just remains to cook your 'olives'. If you don't have a proper oven you could always lightly oil your olives and package them in foil [leaving an opening for water vapour to escape] and place on fire embers, or cook on a griddle. You'll know when they're done.

SPICED PIGEON SOUP

2 pigeons	Butter or oil
Spices	1 pint nettles or other wild greens
2 pints water	Salt
1 onion or spring onion	

• Cut pigeon meat off the bone and then boil the carcasses, along with the giblets, in a couple of pints of water to make a basic stock. • Meanwhile, dice or slice the best meat, then very lightly season with spices and salt, and set aside. • The choice of spice is a personal one - you might want to make it more curry-like or a simple chilli flavour. Another alternative would be some crushed juniper* berries.

• Chop the onion finely or slice the spring onion into small pieces and sauté in some butter or oil until they begin to soften. • Add the sliced pigeon meat to the pan and continue frying until the meat is reasonably well sealed. • Remove from the pan, draining off the oil, and set aside.

• Place the nettle leaves or another wild spinach-like substitute, into the hot pan and wilt the leaves. • Meanwhile, strain the stock into another pan, add the fried onion and meat and bring to the boil. • Add the nettle leaves, and turn down the heat to simmer for 10-15 minutes, or until the meat is very tender.

PHEASANT OR PIGEON BROTH

Pheasant joints or pigeon	Mixed herbs
1 onion	Salt and pepper
Handful pearl barley	1-2 pints chicken stock
2 cups mushrooms - sliced	

Pheasant would be the preferred game fowl for this, but pigeon can be used.

• Remove the meat from the bone and dice into small pieces. • Finely chop the onion and slice the mushrooms. • Place the bones and main ingredients into a pan and bring to the boil for a couple of minutes then cover and simmer very gently until the meat is very tender. • Take off the heat and remove the bones, shredding any meat still on the bone into the broth.

ALTERNATIVES
In the outdoors you may not have access to pearl barley, but there may well be other grains around locally that can be substituted. It's a similar story with the herbs. Also consider adding a few wild pot-herbs.

FISHY & SHELLED THINGS

TANDOORI GRILLED PERCH

1 perch - filleted
Plain yoghurt
2 tbsp. lemon juice
1 onion
Paprika, cayenne, ground cumin
Tomato purée
Salt and pepper

Now for something completely different! Yes, perch is good stuffed and baked, but what about something more imaginative reflecting our love of Indian food?

• To begin with perch is a devil of a fish to gut, clean and trim; it has tough scales and lots of sharp fins. If you cannot face the idea of doing the job yourself you could ask a fishmonger or the angler who caught the fish. If preparing the fish yourself cut off the spiny fins and remove the scales using the boiled water process [*see introductory pages to the recipe section*]. • Once skinned, cut the fillets and place in a shallow dish.

• Put all the sauce ingredients in a bowl, mix together, pour over the fish and leave to marinate for a couple of hours [refrigerate if possible]. • Then put the fillets on a foil-lined grill pan and grill each fillet side under a moderate heat for 5-6 minutes. • Put any sauce remaining in the marinading dish into a small pan and gently heat. Pour over the served fish.

PIKE IN CIDER & CREAM

Pike steaks
Sliced onion
Cider
Cream
Salt and pepper

• Season the pike steaks and place in an oven dish along with a sliced onion and several good slugs of cider. Something like a local scrumpy will impart more interesting flavours than the industrial variety. • Cover and bake for about 30 minutes in a moderate oven. • Then reduce the heat, pour the cream over the steaks, and bake without the lid for another 5 minutes or so.

VARIATIONS

Given the apple connection who not try serving with some apple additions? Thinly sliced or grated cookers perhaps, or even a little jellied or cooked crab-apple. Acidify raw apple with a little lemon if you are worried about cosmetics.

For readers really at a loss on how transform that newly caught pike consider the recipes of our 16th century ancestors which included cooking whole boiled pike with white wine, ginger and cinnamon, and also simmering pike chunks in a sauce comprising apples, lemon juice and paprika. In the 17th century Izaak Walton mentions a recipe that included stuffing pike with its shredded liver mixed with marjoram and savory, then placing this in the cavity with anchovies, mace and orange juice. Garlic was optional!

PIKE WITH MUSTARD SAUCE

Pike - filleted	¼ cup milk
½ pint water	Mustard
1 sliced onion	Lemon juice
Flour	Seasoning
Butter	

With bones bristling like the serried ranks of 'pikes' on a medieval battlefield the pike fish is unfortunately a bony one, but here is one way of cooking it.

• First, fillet the fish keeping its skin [if you have time overnight immerse the fillets in a mixture of vinegar and water [3:1] to soften and even dissolve many of the smaller bones].

• Place the fillets in a pan with the sliced onion and water. • Add seasoning then bring the pan up to simmering point. • When the fish is cooked remove pan from the heat.

• Create a roux in a pan by adding some flour to about a tablespoon of melted butter, stirring constantly to produce a smooth paste. • Cook for about a minute then remove the pan from the heat. • Pour in the cooking liquor from the fish while continuing to stir. • Add the milk and bring the contents of the pan gently to the boil till the liquor thickens then simmer for a few more minutes.

• Now it's time to add a teaspoon of mustard. Here you have several options.... domestic powdered, ready-made, or the seeds and crushed leaves of plants in the wild. If you are contemplating the latter the common hedge mustard*, and black* or white mustard are your best options.

• Take some of the cooking liquid and mix in your chosen mustard and a little lemon juice. • Add this to the larger bulk of the sauce, stir in and season to taste. Pour over the fish and serve.

GARLIC BREAM

Bream [freshwater variety]
Oil
Alexanders - stalk and leaves [or celery]
3-4 garlic cloves [or ramsons]
Lemon juice
½ cup water

Bream is a bony fish without a great deal of flavour and can be muddy, but if you catch one here's a recipe to tackle it.

• Crush the garlic cloves, chop the alexanders and then combine with oil [preferably olive to impart more taste], lemon juice, several good pinches of salt, and a pinch of pepper. • Stuff the fish with some of this mixture. • Place the fish in a greased baking dish, make deep diagonal incisions in the upper side of the fish and smother it with the remainder of the mixture. • Add the water and then bake for 30 minutes in a moderate oven, or until done.

VARIATIONS
Replace the garlic with heaps of oregano or rosemary. You might consider serving it with a sorrel* sauce too [see note in Wild Plant Reference section].

CHINESE FRESHWATER FISH BALLS

2-3 cups uncooked fish
1 cup cornflour
1 egg
Sesame oil [others will do]
Spring onions
1 tbsp. vinegar
Ginger
Garlic clove
Salt and pepper

This recipe adds a Chinese twist to fish balls. • Mince or finely chop the raw fish and place in a bowl with some seasoning, crushed garlic and grated ginger. • Mix in the cornflour and the egg and roll into 1-inch sized balls. • Drop the balls into boiling stock [preferably fish] to which a splash of vinegar and a slug of sesame or other oil have been added. They should cook in about 5 minutes.

ALTERNATIVES
Deep-fry the fish balls and serve with a sweet and sour sauce. Incidentally, an ancient Chinese recipe mixed chrysanthemum flowers with dace. Might be worth experimenting with other fragrant flowers and dace in a type of fishcake or fish ball.

FISH WITH BROOM PICKLES

1 medium onion
Butter or oil
Filleted fish
1 cup sour cream
1 tbsp. broom* pickles
Salt and pepper

This is one way of trying to cook with those broom pickles that you might have prepared during the year. This is a very sauce-like recipe which is best served over boiled, or baked potatoes, or even rice.

• Finely slice the onion and sauté until the pieces just begin to soften. • Add small-ish chunks of skinned, filleted fish - one of the better freshwater eating fish - to the pan. • Add seasoning then stir in the sour cream a bit at a time, followed by the broom pickles. • Thoroughly mix the ingredients then put in a greased baking dish and cook in a preheated moderate oven for about 20-30 minutes.

PERCH or PIKE CEVICHE

Fresh perch / bream fillet
2 large lemons [limes preferred]
Red chilli pepper [preferred]
Salt and pepper
Oil
Tomatoes

'Cev what? Isn't that something to do with golf?' Not likely.

This dish is derived from the method of cooking fresh fish simply through the acidic action of lemon or lime juice. If you cannot lay your hands on a small 'real' chilli pepper don't resort to the powdered type as that really does not do justice to the taste of the lemon-cooked fish. Similarly, use real lemons and not the bottled chemical type.

• Slice the fresh fish fillet across its length into ¼-inch thick pieces. • Place on a plate or glass dish and squeeze over the lemon juice. • Use your fingers to make sure the fish pieces are coated all over with the juice. • Cover and set aside for about an hour while the fish 'cooks'. • Meanwhile, chop the red chilli finely. • De-seed the tomatoes and also chop into small pieces – as a very simple salsa-type accompaniment – and lightly season. • Once 'cooked' sprinkle the chopped chilli over the fish, season and dribble some oil over too [it really has to be olive oil to do the fish justice] then gently mix through with your fingers. • Leave for another 30 minutes. • Serve with the chopped tomatoes.

GINGER CARP

1 carp [or chosen alternative]
Root ginger
½ cup fish stock
Sugar or clear honey
Basil and rosemary
Hazelnuts or pine nuts

• Grate about a teaspoon of ginger root and add to the cup of stock, along with a teaspoon of sugar or honey [takes the edge off the ginger], a sprinkling of the herbs and roughly chopped nuts. • Stir the mixture well together and set aside.

• Put the cleaned and prepared carp onto a piece of baking foil large enough to wrap the fish and which has been lightly oiled, and place in a baking dish. • Pour over the liquid and place in a moderate pre-heated oven and bake till cooked - about 20-30 minutes depending on fish size. Serve the flavoured cooking juices poured over the fish.

ALTERNATIVES
Something else you might like to try is trout cooked with the cavity stuffed with rice, butter and ginger, then simply placed in a preheated oven till cooked and browned.

Another option is to stuff the carp with a mixture of chopped walnuts, some finely chopped onions, chopped tomatoes, pinches of paprika and cinnamon, and seasoning. For an oriental style variation, drop the herbs, honey and nuts, and replace with spring onions to complement the ginger flavour.

Also try frying carp and serving with a sauce of creamed horseradish and chopped watercress, or baking carp with [crushed] caraway seeds. If you have a spirit of culinary adventure, one 16th century recipe for carp bakes a buttered fish with nutmeg, raisins and orange juice. In the 17th century Izaak Walton went one better with a stuffing of '*twenty pickled oysters, and three anchovies,*' then added claret, salt, cloves, mace, orange rind and lemons and 'boiled' the fish on a fire.

CURRIED PIKE BALLS

2 cups pike meat - ground
White bread
Salt
1 egg
Pinch curry powder [or spices of choice]
Fine meal or flour
Butter or oil

• Crumble two crustless slices of white bread into crumbs and add to about 2 cups of ground pike meat in a bowl. • Add a good pinch of salt, your chosen curry spices, and the egg. • Mix thoroughly and form into 1-inch balls. • Dip these into the meal or flour and fry in the butter.

SWEET CICELY FISH CAKES

Sweet cicely roots
Fish - raw
Small onion
2 handfuls breadcrumbs
1-2 eggs
Salt and pepper
Oil

• Peel the parsnip alternative sweet cicely roots, slice and then boil until tender enough to mash. • Drain, cool and mash. • Mince your chosen fish then place in a bowl with the finely chop the onion, egg, breadcrumbs and some seasoning. • Add the sweet cicely mash and mix together well. • Heat some oil in a frying pan and spoon in dollops of the mixture, patting down to flatten out. • Cook for 3-4 minutes on each side.

CHESTNUT FISH CAKES

Fish – uncooked mashed
Chestnuts – mashed
Chilli powder [optional]
Salt
Egg yolk [optional]
Butter or oil

In the endeavour to provide recipes from the far side, here's another one. The proportion of mashed fish to mashed chestnuts is 1:1. The fish is one of your choice but one of the quality freshwater species is most preferred. The fish cakes will just about maintain their shape without the addition of egg yolk in case you have none to hand, but are very fragile [don't make them more than 3 inches wide in that case].

• Take raw fish meat and mash roughly with a fork. • Similarly mash some cooked chestnuts, trying to make sure there are no large lumps left. • Combine the fish and chestnut and mix thoroughly, adding seasoning and the chilli spice if required. • Finally stir in the egg yolk – about 1 yolk per cup of final mixture – if you are going down this route. • Mix thoroughly then form into small flat patties. • Fry in a little oil – the first side for 2-3 minutes before turning the repeat on the other side.

ALTERNATIVES

The fish content of the recipe can be increased but then the resulting fish cakes tend to be extremely flaky and fragile. In the absence of any egg as a binder there is always the possibility of adding some flour or some bread soaked in milk – and then squeezed almost dry - to the fish-chestnut mixture.

The author likes to prepare these fish cakes in their natural state rather than adulterate with spices. In so doing there opens up a host of sauces or accompaniments that you might like to serve alongside. For example, a salsa of red chilli peppers and tomatoes – complementing the slightly sweet chestnut ingredient. Of course, this is ultimately down to availability.

SALMON FISH CAKES

Salmon meat
Rice – cooked
Egg yolk
Flour
Salt and pepper
Butter or oil

This recipe can use fresh uncooked salmon or make use of any leftovers. Use proportions of 1:1 salmon and rice, and one egg yolk and a level tablespoon of flour per cupful of mixture.

• Very quickly flake the salmon meat. • Mash [or roughly blend] the rice. • Place these ingredients in a bowl with the egg, flour and seasoning. • Mix thoroughly together with a fork, making sure to break up any larger pieces of salmon. • Form into flat patties and then fry for 3-4 minutes on each side.

SPICY PIKE SAUSAGE

2-3 cups pike fillet / meat	½ cup flour or meal [optional]
2-3 slices bread	Breadcrumbs [optional]
¼-½ cup milk	Paprika [optional]
1 tbsp. sage	Butter or oil [optional]
2 eggs	Salt and pepper

This recipe provides two options for the cooking method, so read on...

• Begin by wetting the bread slices with some milk, and allow to soak in. • Meanwhile, coarsely mash the pike meat with a fork [other good quality freshwater fish can also be used] and place in a bowl. • Squeeze out the milk soaked bread, break into pieces and add to the bowl along with a tablespoon of chosen herbs that complement fish [see *Quick Herb Guide for your options*], seasoning and 1 egg. • Mix together thoroughly then form into 1-inch thick sausages.

The next stage is where you have two options on the cooking method. • First, the preferred spicy fried version.... • Add a large pinch of paprika [more if you like 'heat'] to some flour. • Beat the second egg. • Dip your pike sausages in the flour or meal, then coat with beaten egg and dunk in breadcrumbs. • Finally, shallow fry in butter or oil until nicely browned.

• The second cooking method provides you with different ways of cooking your pike sausage depending on circumstances, but essentially it involves baking or boiling the sausages in individual kitchen foil wraps, but leaving out the spice ingredients [this will certainly give your chosen herb content a key flavouring role].

• Very lightly oil one side of a piece of foil and place your sausage at one end. • Roll the foil package up – making sure the foil overlaps at least one time - and twist the ends to seal. • If you have an oven place the packages in a preheated moderate to moderately-hot oven and cook for about 25 minutes. • Alternatively, cook in boiling water for about 15-20 minutes.

FISH AND CRAB-APPLE CURRY

Fish fillets
Plain flour
1 onion
1-2 handfuls crab-apples
Lemon juice
Butter or oil
Curry powder [or spices of choice]
Water or stock
Dried fruits
Cornflour

You have caught yourself a magnificent specimen from the nearest lake, but what to do with it other than fry? How about trying to curry it along these lines...?

• Sprinkle the fillets [quantity depending on hunger levels] with salt, cut into pieces and dip in the flour and gently fry so that both sides are slightly browned then remove from the heat. • Slice the onion. • Halve the crab-apples and remove the core parts, then slice again [ie. each apple quartered]. • Place in a bowl of water to reduce browning.

• Put butter or oil in a pan and heat, adding the curry powder and the onion. • Fry until the onion softens then add the apple segments and cook for a few minutes, before adding the about a pint of water [vegetable or fish stock will be more tasty] and a handful of whatever dried fruits you can find. Elderberries, currants, sultanas or apricots for example. • Add the fish.

• The curry needs thickening so mix about a tablespoon of cornflour with some of the liquor then stir in. • Bring to the boil then simmer. Somewhere between 10 and 15 minutes should do it, but you want to make sure the fish doesn't disintegrate. Season to taste and serve.

SALMON OR TROUT KEDGEREE

Trout or salmon fillet
1 small onion
1 large tbsp. butter
1 tsp. turmeric
3 cups cooked rice
2 hard-boiled eggs
Salt and pepper
Cayenne or paprika [optional]

Memsahib, another way to serve up that trout your other half caught this morning. Since trout or salmon meat are tasty but delicate, and kedgeree is normally made in the UK with smoked haddock which imparts its own unique flavour, this adaptation hots things up a little with spices.

• Begin by poaching the fillets [still with the skin on] in a little water for about 10 minutes, or until cooked. • Remove from the heat, drain, then skin and flake the meat.

• Put the chopped onion in a frying pan and sauté in butter till the onion softens. • Then stir in the turmeric and continue cooking for another minute. • Stir in the rice and fish, and add seasoning plus the optional sprinkle of cayenne or paprika. • While the mixture continues to cook chop the hard-boiled eggs then add to the pan and mix in thoroughly. Serve.

SPICED RIVER TROUT

Whole trout
Allspice
Salt and pepper
Spring onions
Bacon

• To a little salt and pepper add several pinches of allspice [or alternatives below], and mix together. • Make diagonal cuts in the skin of the trout. • Rub the mixture in the fish cavity and over the exterior surface. • Slice a couple of spring onions along their length and also insert into the cavity. • To hold the stuffing in place wrap the fish with a couple of bacon rashers. • The fish can then be baked, grilled or cooked over a campfire until the flesh flakes.

ALTERNATIVES
The allspice can be replaced by pinches of ground cloves, cinnamon and nutmeg.

GRAYLING VINDALOO

Grayling
½ tsp. cayenne, turmeric, ground coriander, black pepper, hot mustard powder
1 tsp. cumin
Ground ginger and cinnamon - good pinches.
1 tsp. salt
Vinegar
Oil
Water

Goa meets downtown Dorset... or any other corner of the wilderness.

There are two methods here of cooking your gutted and cleaned grayling, depending on the cooking facilities you have available.

• For readers with a cooker put the fish under a grill and just lightly cook the surface until the skin can be removed. • Then place the fish on some lightly oiled foil in a baking dish, and pour over the sauce. • Lightly crimp the foil and place the dish in a moderately hot oven and bake until done.

Basic cooking can be accomplished with a campfire too. Don't worry about scaling as the skin can be carefully removed after cooking while the vindaloo sauce will certainly have done its work flavouring and permeating the flesh.

• Score the fish on both sides with cuts about ¼-inch deep. • Place the fish on a double thickness of oiled foil and then smear some of the sauce in the cavity, and over both sides of the fish. • Fold the foil into an envelope and lightly crimp the edges to prevent juices running out. • Place on a grill over hot embers. • Cook until the flesh flakes - checking progress from time to time. • When done, carefully remove the skin, serve the fish and spoon vindaloo sauce over. Cooking this way will provide more of a steamed or braised fish than with the previous oven method.

• To prepare the cooking sauce, put measures of the spices and salt in a small dish and stir in a little vinegar to make a paste. • Place some oil in a small pan, heat and add the spice paste. • Reduce the heat so that the spices don't burn.

- Cook the spices for about 5 minutes, stirring rapidly to prevent sticking.
- Add a little water to thin the sauce if you wish. • Take off the heat and set aside for smothering the fish later.

SWEET n SPICY CAMPFIRE FISH

Fish fillets
Maple syrup or clear honey
Allspice
Salt and pepper
Butter or oil

This is another way you might like to cook a filleted trout - but more particularly a less tasty or inspiring freshwater fish.

• Mix together the salt, pepper and allspice [or alternatives below]. • Pour some maple syrup or clear honey on the bottom of a plate and coat the fillets. • Sprinkle the fillets with the seasoning mix and then skewer the fillets lengthwise, or place on a rack and broil over the fire, or grill. • Depending on fillet size cooking times will be about 2-5 minutes. • Baste with the remaining syrup or honey during cooking.

ALTERNATIVES
The allspice can be replaced by pinches of ground cloves, cinnamon and nutmeg.

JUNIPER SALMON & CHICKWEED SALAD

Salmon steak
Juniper* berries
Butter or oil
Salt and pepper
Stock or water [optional]
Chickweed

Try explaining it to the neighbours... picking chickweed for the kitchen.

• Coarsely crush half a dozen juniper berries. • Lightly oil the salmon steaks and press the flat surfaces into the crushed junipers [a similar action to preparing steak au poivres], and season lightly. • Heat some oil or butter in a frying pan and cook the salmon steaks for 3-4 minutes on each side [or grille until the meat is flaky]. • Remove from the heat, skin the steaks, and allow to partly cool before flaking the meat. • Place in a bowl with some tender chickweed and mix through. • Add a little water to the frying pan, heat and stir round to absorb the flavours – adding a little more oil or butter in addition, if required. • Drizzle the liquor over the salad [strain off berries if you find them too bitter] and serve.

FRIED EEL

Eel
Egg
Breadcrumbs
Salt and pepper
Butter or oil

Here are two simple ways of cooking eel. • In both cases split the skinned eel and cut it into 3 or 4-inch pieces ready for either cooking method.

• In version one dip the pieces into beaten egg, coat in breadcrumbs and then fry in oil or butter. • The second version simply requires the eel to be dipped into flour before frying.

VARIATION
Instead of breadcrumbs try oatmeal as an alternative.

EEL BAKE

2-3 cups eel
1 pint fish or vegetable stock
1 cup water
3-4 pints nettle or fat hen leaves
Onion
Butter and oil
1 tbsp. broom* pickles, or capers
1 cup breadcrumbs
Salt and pepper

• Cut the boned and skinned eel fillet into 1-2 inch chunks, then simmer in the stock for a few minutes. • Remove eel from the liquid, reserving a cup of the stock but then topping up with the cup of water to replace.

• Bring the liquid in the pan to the boil and add the nettle leaves to the pan.
• Blanche for a couple of minutes then remove the leaves and drain.

• Meanwhile slice the onion lengthwise and sauté in a pan until the onion begins to soften. • Add the cup of stock kept behind and turn up the heat to bring to boiling. • Add nettles leaves and allow to cook for a minute before turning down the heat to very low. • Cover and allow to cook for 10 minutes, then add seasoning.

• Place half of the cooked leaves in the bottom of an ovenproof dish. • Layer the eel pieces over this and sprinkle over the broom pickles, then the remaining cooked leaves and any remaining stock or cooking juices. • Sprinkle on the breadcrumbs and drizzle a little melted butter over. • Place in a preheated moderately-hot oven and bake for another 20-30 minutes.

GRILLED / BBQ EEL

Eels
Dark soy sauce
Sugar
Root ginger - grated
Salt and pepper

• Split the eel and open out along the spine. • Make a marinade from the other ingredients and soak the eel for an hour.

• Place the eel on a grill with the skin facing heat source and cook until the skin is crispy. • Turn over and cook the other side till done.

ALTERNATIVES

For eel with a difference, how about currying your catch? As a proper curry - perhaps a variation on the FISH AND CRAB-APPLE CURRY recipe or even the WILD CRAYFISH GUMBO creation. Even more simply, lightly oil the meat and sprinkle with a little mild curry powder or garam masala and grill.

BRAISED EELS

Eel - skinned
Oil
Soy sauce
Water [stock preferred]
Alexanders - blanched stems [or celery]
2 garlic cloves [or ramsoss]
Cornflour
Vinegar

That's *braised*... and *not* in the welding sense!

• Cut your prepared eels into 2-inch pieces, then fry for about 5 minutes ensuring all parts are touched by the heat. • Add a couple of slugs of soy sauce, a cup of water or stock, the whole garlic cloves, and thinly sliced, blanched alexanders stems. • Cover and simmer for about 10 minutes. • Mix a little cornflour with some water and add this to the pan with a splash of vinegar. • Simmer for another few minutes or until the cornflour has started to thicken.

ALTERNATIVES

For something completely different to do with eels, gently stew them for about 30 minutes in beer or pale ale with bay leaves, sage and a whole clove of garlic.

SPICY EEL BROTH

Eel
Salt
Butter or oil
Ginger, cinnamon, cloves
1½-2 pints water or fish stock
Lemon juice
1-2 cups rice or other grain - pre-cooked

• Cut the skinned and gutted eel into 1-inch chunks, season with salt and then fry to seal the meat. • Remove eel pieces from the pan and heat the spices in the remaining oil. • Return the eel pieces to the pan. • Add water or fish stock, rice and a slug of lemon juice. • Bring to the boil and simmer until the eel is very tender.

WILD CRAYFISH

Crayfish
Water
Herbs or spices

The British native freshwater crayfish - the White Clawed Crayfish - is an 'endangered species' and is under pressure from a much larger escapee cousin called the Signal Crayfish, which can easily reach 6 inches in length. Our indigenous one rarely grows beyond 4 inches and is protected by law. Even if that were not the case give our humble native ones a sporting chance and eat the predatory signal crayfish, and if you do catch a native one return it to its watery home.

Crayfish are cooked live, just like lobster. • Clean them first under running water. • Then drop the crayfish in boiling water, cover the pan, and cook for 3-7 minutes depending on the crayfish size. • If you want to impart a herby or spicy flavour to the cooked meat then you may add something like dill or chilli to the cooking water.

• To get at the best meat - in the tail - allow the crayfish to cool then take hold of the head and end of the tail, twist in opposite directions and pull gently to separate. • Pinch the bottom of the tail with your fingers to loosen up the meat and extract the meat in one piece. • The black vein you can see is the intestine.

Remove with a sharp knife tip and discard. • Quickly rinse the meat and it is ready to eat, or to include in another dish...

ALTERNATIVES
If you like pasta, why not try making ravioli with a crayfish filling? Make that by chopping cooked crayfish, then mashing with a few fresh breadcrumbs, some seasoning and herbs, a little cream and some egg. Go lightly on the cream, and add a few more breadcrumbs if the mixture becomes wet. If you have any mushrooms, serve your crayfish ravioli with a mushroom sauce.

WILD CRAYFISH GUMBO

2 tbsp. oil and flour
1 onion
1 cup chopped celery or wild equivalent
2-3 garlic cloves
1 can tomatoes
2 cups of water [or fish stock]
1 pint cooked crayfish meat
Salt and pepper
Pinch sugar
Chilli powder [optional]

Nope, this is not a true gumbo - which should have red bell peppers and okra among the ingredients - but an approximation to liven up your prepared crayfish.

• The onion, celery and garlic all need to be chopped. • Next make a roux with the flour and oil.... Heat the oil over a low heat and add the flour gradually, stirring in briskly. • Cook very slowly until the roux is a nutty brown colour.

• Stir in the chopped onions, garlic and chopped celery and cook until they begin to soften - again, slowly. • Add the water or fish stock to the roux, stir thoroughly and bring to the boil. • Add seasoning, chilli and a pinch of sugar. • Keep on a very low heat and cook for another 20-30 minutes before adding the canned tomatoes and crayfish. • Cook slowly for another 30-40 minutes, or until the crayfish is tender.

VARIATIONS
Alexanders stems or similar could be used to replace the chopped celery stalks. The canned tomatoes can be dropped if you cannot find any, while you might like to try adding some equivalent of bell peppers if you happen to be cooking this at home or have access to a local supermarket.

WILD CRAYFISH PILAF

Cooked rice	4 tbsp. flour
1 onion	2 cups milk
Crayfish meat - cooked	Butter or oil
Greens [optional]	Salt and pepper

• Chop the onion finely and slice the crayfish meat into mouthful-size pieces, then mix together with the rice and any 'prepared' chopped greens you wish to add. • Grease or oil a baking dish and fill with the mixture.

• Put the flour into a bowl, add a couple of tablespoons of melted butter, the milk and some seasoning to produce a white sauce which is then poured over the rice and meat mixture. • Bake in a moderate oven for about 30 minutes.

VARIATIONS
The 'greens' above could be anything from a green pepper if you have one, to celery or the stems of alexanders, or nettles. You might also consider whether you want to add a hint of curry powder or spices for variety.

FISH GOULASH

Fish fillet
Onions
Garlic cloves
Butter or oil
Paprika
Wild stem greens or roots [optional]
Fish stock
Canned tomatoes
Tomato purée
Salt and pepper

The previous gumbo recipe sort of inspired the idea for making a goulash out of your freshwater catch. Ideally the fish wants to be one of the better ones like perch or carp. Amounts of ingredients are left deliberately vague allowing circumstances to dictate. However, the paprika is essential!

• Cut the skinned fillet into good mouth sized pieces. • Thinly slice some onion and crush the garlic, then sauté gently until the onion is softened along with pinches of paprika.

• Add the fish to the pan [if you wish to add some wild stem or root vegetable ingredient do so now - but these need to be cooked until just tender]. • Pour in fish or vegetable stock, keeping a little aside with which to thin the tomato purée. • Add this to the pan too, plus some tomatoes – canned will do if you are in the wilds – and seasoning. • Stir well, then cover the pan and reduce to a gentle heat and cook for 10-15 minutes, or until the fish is done. • However, don't stir the pan's contents as the fish will break up.

VARIATIONS
The fish stock for this recipe can come from what is left of your catch after the filleting process; ensuring you make the best use of everything.

FRESHWATER FISH PIE

2-3 large potatoes	2 tbsp. butter
Fish meat	Flour
Butter	Milk
Milk	Salt and pepper
Salt and pepper	

• Begin by boiling peeled potatoes until they are tender. • Meanwhile take skinned, boned fish and cut into good sized chunks. • Once the potatoes are done, drain, mash and add a good chunk of butter, a little warmed milk and seasoning. • Mix together.

• Make a simple white sauce by adding flour to some melted butter in a pan then adding enough milk and stirring to form a smooth sauce - enough to cover the fish. • Add seasoning to taste. • Place the fish in an ovenproof dish, pour the sauce over, and layer the mashed potato on top. • Place in a moderate oven and bake for about 50-60 minutes.

STUFFED ZANDER

Zander - whole
Onion
Chicken - cooked
Bacon or ham - cooked
Butter or oil
2 eggs

What better way to deal with this voracious fish than to give it a right good stuffing. With flaky white flesh the zander can grow very large. Choose a smaller one for this recipe.

• Finely chop the onion, dice the chicken leftovers small, and also the bacon or ham. • Gently fry these in some butter or oil. • Break two eggs and stir into the pan, distributing through the mixture. • Once the egg has cooked, remove pan from the heat and stuff the zander with the mixture. • Place in a baking dish, cover with foil and cook in a moderate oven until the fish is done.

VARIATIONS

For a slightly more savoury variation create a stuffing with chopped mushrooms, onions and olives, a sliced hot pepper, and mixed with some oil and a drizzle of vinegar.

ZANDER & CHEESED GREENS

Zander fillets
2 cups good king henry leaves
Butter and oil
Flour
Milk
Parmesan

- Gently simmer the zander fillets in some salted water until almost done.
- Drain off the water and place the fillets into a lightly oiled ovenproof dish.

- Meanwhile, gently wilt the green leaves in a little butter. • When softened cover the zander fillets with the greens. • The next stage is to make the cheese sauce which is a **basic béchamel sauce** with cheese added. • Grate the cheese and set aside. • Put 2 level tablespoons of butter in a thick-based pan and melt at a low heat. • Gradually stir in 2-3 tablespoons of flour - the amount depending on the sauce thickness required. • Keep the mixture cooking for a couple of minutes then add ½ pint of milk a bit at a time while continuing to stir. [A similar volume of liquid made up of cream or fish stock with the milk can be used.] • Raise the heat slightly and continue stirring until the sauce thickens. • Add the grated cheese and some seasoning, and continue cooking until the parmesan has melted.

- Pour the cheese sauce over the zander and leaf greens. • Drizzle a little olive oil over, or dot a couple of small knobs of butter on top. • Place in a hot oven and cook for about 10-15 minutes.

VARIATIONS

You can vary the type of cheese used, but it should preferably be a hard one. The good king henry or other wild leaves can be replaced with spinach. The basic béchamel can have other ingredients added to it – broom* capers or mushrooms for example.

GUDGEON IN WINE

Gudgeon
White wine - preferably sweet
Ginger
Spring onion [optional]

Sugar [if using dry wine]
Salt

Being a generally small fish of sardine size it seemed appropriate to treat them more delicately and add a little piquant twist. That said, the gudgeon has large-ish scales which are best removed - by the hot water method for simplicity.

• Place the fish in a lightly oiled oven dish, add a glass of sweet white wine, and a few slivers of ginger root sliced finely. • If you wish to add finely sliced spring onion do so now, but on your first time out with this dish try without. • Cook in a moderate oven till done. • Remove the fish and reduce the cooking liquor to pour over as a sauce, seasoning as required.

ALTERNATIVES
How about a much more bold tasting recipe to inspire you...? Put the prepared gudgeon in an oven dish then sieve some plum tomatoes over the top, add some very finely chopped onions, and a good slug of port. Again, bake in a moderate oven till done. Readers cooking over a campfire could simply simmer the fish very gently, then separately reduce the cooking liquor.

CHARGRILLED CHAR & PINE NUTS

Char steaks
Bacon
Pine nuts
Butter and oil
Cider vinegar
Salt and pepper

Just because it is called char that doesn't mean you should do a King Alfred on this recipe. Char reach about 10-12 inches in length so the 'steaks' are not large.

• Lightly season the steaks, and brush or smear with oil. • Place in a very hot frying pan or on a griddle, and cook for about 3-4 minutes on each side. • Remove from the heat and set aside.

• To make the sauce chop the bacon and fry in another pan for several minutes before adding some pine nuts [since many pines have small nuts, apart from the Stone Pine, you might prefer to buy some ready-prepared pine kernels]. • Turn down the heat and continue to cook for about a minute, making sure not to burn the nuts. • Remove from the heat, add a knob of soft butter and stir till it melts, then add a splash of a good vinegar and briskly mix. • Serve the sauce over your 'steaks'.

FRESHWATER BOUILLABAISSE

1 large onion
1 leek
2 skinned tomatoes
1-2 garlic cloves
Oil
Sprigs of fennel, thyme and parsley
2 pints boiling water
Saffron
2-3 lb of mixed fish [gudgeon, common bream, dace, pike, zander]
Salt and pepper
1 or 2 large boiled potatoes or toast

Some folks are awfully sniffy about the interpretation of the recipes used for the original Provençal fish soup which is regarded as one of the classics of cooking. However, if you have an adventurous mind, and don't care a hoot in hades about convention, why not try to conjure up a freshwater equivalent rather than baking, grilling or frying your catch?

• Clean and bone your fish and cut into good sized chunks. • Chop the onion and leek finely, crush the garlic, quarter the tomatoes and place all of this in a pan with a good slug of oil [preferably olive oil given the mediterranean provenance of bouillabaise] plus the herbs, and fry for a few minutes. • Stir in the boiling water while continuing to boil over the heat for another couple of minutes. • Add a pinch of saffron if available, some seasoning and your fish chunks. • Simmer for about 10 minutes.

• To serve, put the fish pieces in the bottom of the bowl with some of the vegetables, then pour over the soup. Serve with toast or some boiled potatoes.

ALTERNATIVES
Since the source of your main ingredients here are freshwater lakes and rivers there is a good possibility that reeds and arrowhead are available and the cooked roots of these could be an interesting substitute for the potatoes.

FRESHWATER FISH PUDDING

Cooked fish meat
1 onion
Oil
1 cup breadcrumbs
Milk
Salt and pepper
Eggs

The origins of this recipe lie with Portuguese cooking, and it was thought that it could provide a very different way of treating your catch.

• Essentially you can use any cooked fish meat which is then minced or chopped finely. • Also finely chop a small onion and sauté in olive oil [preferred] until lightly browned. • Then add the fish to the pan plus some seasoning.

• Beat 2 or 3 eggs and set aside. • Then, in a separate pan, add a handful of breadcrumbs and boil in a cup of milk. • Take off the heat and combine the fish and onion with the milk and bread mixture, stir, and then pour in the beaten eggs. • Continue to stir – adding a little more milk if the mixture becomes too stiff [but don't make it very runny]. • Pour into a buttered or lightly oiled baking dish and cook in a moderate oven for 45 minutes to an hour, or until done.

FRESHWATER FISH PUDDING #2

1-1½ cups white fish meat - cubed
Handful white bread – cubed
1-2 cups milk
Onion - small
Butter or oil
3-4 eggs
Salt and pepper

Unlike the previous recipe which is more quiche-like in its texture, the following dish is much lighter, using beaten egg whites to this end.

• Separate the eggs into yolks and whites. • Cube the fish and bread into sugar lump sized pieces then soak the bread in the milk. • Finely chop the onion and sauté until softened. • Remove from the heat and add the fish, soaked bread and yolks to the pan, season, and combine thoroughly. • Beat the egg whites until they stiffen then fold into the pan mixture *gently* – the idea is to keep the air in the egg whites.

• Place the mixture into a lightly greased oven dish, cover with some lightly greased foil, and place in a preheated moderate oven and cook for about 30-40 minutes or until the mixture is set – exact time will depend on depth of mixture in the dish. • Remove from the oven and allow to rest for a few minutes before serving.

FRESHWATER FISH STEW

Various filleted fish of choice
Fish stock
White wine
½ cup lovage* or cuckooflower or hairy bittercress leaves
Coriander - ground
Cornflour
Oregano
Pepper

• Slice the fish into roughly 1-inch pieces. • Place in an oven dish with the lovage* or other peppery wild leaves, some ground coriander, oil, and enough stock and wine to cover. • Place in a pre-heated moderate oven and cook till done. • Remove, and pour off the cooking liquor into a pan. • Add some cornflour which has been mixed with a little water and stir into the liquor. • Raise the heat and cook until the liquid thickens. • Return the fish to the pan, sprinkle over some coriander, a pinch of pepper and simmer for a few minutes before serving.

FRESHWATER FISH STEW 2

Bacon
Onions
Butter or oil
Potatoes
Fish stock and/or milk or water
Filleted fish
Salt and pepper

This is another of those recipes stripped down to barest essentials with the quantities of ingredients left entirely to personal taste, circumstance or degree of hunger. Use a good quality freshwater fish.

• Slice the onions and dice the bacon, then lightly fry both in a pan - just until the onion softens. • Add diced [sugar lump size] or sliced potato and stir in. • Cover the pan and continue cooking until the outside of the potato pieces just begins to soften. • Season the mixture then add the liquid - to a level just below the surface of the potatoes. • Place pieces of filleted fish on top, then cover and cook slowly until the potatoes are done - about 20-30 minutes.

FISH & WATERCRESS TERRINE

Perch or grayling meat
Trout or salmon meat

2-3 slices white bread – crumbed
2 eggs
2 handfuls watercress*
Cream
Salt and pepper
Butter or oil

Don't let the word terrine mystify you, simply regard this recipe as a way of cooking two different types of fish in a small bread loaf tin.

• Begin by removing the thicker stems from the watercress and chop the leaves very finely, then set aside. • Crumb the pieces of bread and set aside.

• Next, remove all the bones you can find in the raw fish meat then, keeping the different fish types separate, cut into pieces and mash with a fork along with some seasoning. • If you have a blender it will make things easier. • Place the minced fish in two separate bowls.

• To the contents of each bowl add a slug of cream, an egg and a handful of the breadcrumbs. • Mix these together so a paste forms [again a blender is ideal].

• Very lightly oil or grease your loaf tin [oiled kitchen foil is another option] then spoon in the salmon or trout mixture and level off as best you can with the back of a spoon.

• Split the whiter fish mixture in half and add the finely chopped watercress to one portion. • Combine thoroughly and layer into the loaf tin. • Finally, add the last of the fish mixture as the top layer. • Cover the top of the tin with a lightly greased piece of foil, put in a baking tray filled with enough boiling water to half fill, then place in a preheated moderate to moderately-hot oven and cook for about 1½ hours, or until done [cooking time will ultimately depend on the depth and thickness of mixtures in the loaf tin. • When cooked allow to cool before turning out of the tin.

FRESHWATER FISH PÂTÉ

Cooked fish remainders [perch, pike, bream, zander]
Butter
Creamed horseradish
Salt and pepper

• Mash, or preferably blend, together one part of butter to two parts of cooked flesh of the better freshwater fish. • Season with salt and pepper, and mix in a small amount of creamed horseradish to give this pâté a piquancy and kick. • Alternatively you could add spices instead. • Chill to set and serve with toast, or with a green salad.

DEVILLED BACON ROACH

Roach fillet - minced
Bacon rashers
Butter or oil
Tomatoes - seeded - or purée
Brown sugar
Lemon juice
Worcestershire sauce
Stock or water

Though the roach has quite firm flesh it tends to be very bony, and the preparation method of this recipe should deal with any small ones that still remain after initial boning.

• Remove as many of the bones as possible and then simply chop or mash the flesh [remove any more bones you happen to find]. • Add seasoning, mix through and set aside.

• Melt some butter in a pan and add some seeded tomatoes and cook till soft - or simply opt for tomato purée straight off. • Add several good sprinkles of sugar [preferably brown], a slug of lemon juice and a good splash of Worcestershire sauce. • Continue cooking, stirring all the ingredients together. • Add some stock or water to thin the devilled sauce - just enough to produce a consistency that coats the back of a spoon. • Take off the heat.

• Form the mashed fish into small sausage-like strips and place on rashers of bacon. • Roll up the bacon. • Depending on cooking circumstances place on a lightly oiled grilling or oven dish. • Smother with the devilled sauce and place the bacon-fish rolls under the grill, or in a hot oven, and cook until done.

FRESHWATER FISH STOCK

Fish trimmings or whole fish
1 onion
Leeks
Fennel
2 pints of water
White wine [optional]
Salt and pepper

Fish stock can be a useful way of using all those unused trimmings from the fish dishes you prepare - for example the head and bones of the pike used in these recipes. It is also possible to use whole fish of species which do not make very good eating in normal circumstances. Chub and rudd, for example. In all cases the fish should be gutted and the blood washed out.

• Chop the vegetables and place in a pan with some sprigs of fennel and the water. • If you decide to add a glass of wine, reduce the water by an equivalent amount. • Bring to the boil slowly and stir, removing any scum that forms on the surface. • Add seasoning to taste, then simmer gently for 30 minutes. Resist cooking for more than 30 minutes since the bones can impart a bitter taste. • Sieve or strain.

SPICY MINNOW FRIES

Minnows
Eggs
Flour or fine meal
Cayenne or curry powder / herbs
Butter or oil

This is a variation on a cooking method mentioned by Isaak Walton in the 17th century when minnows were a popular dish. Adult brethren reach a maximum size of 3 inches or so, and they can be caught either by netting [they usually float around our waters in small shoals] or by angling. A somewhat tedious process given their size.

• Remove the head and guts of these little freshwater sardines, dip into beaten egg and then roll in flour or meal which has been seasoned with a bit of cayenne or curry powder [or herbs if you prefer a herby accent]. • You have the option of frying in a pan or deep-frying. Use the tail to pick up your fried minnows but don't consume.

ALTERNATIVES
Another idea you might like to try with minnows is to bake them in small pastry envelopes. Prepare the minnows as before but remove most of the backbone and the tail. Wrap each minnow in a piece of rolled pastry and bake in a hot oven. Serve as an unusual appetizer.

DULSE & POTATO SOUP

½ cup dulse
1 large potato
1- 1 ½ pints water
3-4 tomatoes - or canned

This is a nice thick soup for cold days. In the absence of tomatoes a squidge of tomato purée could be used to provide that flavour instead. The addition of some fish or shellfish content is another option open to you.

• Rinse the dulse, then soak in water for 10 minutes before cutting into small pieces. • Meanwhile, slice the potato and place in a pan with the water. • Bring to the boil and simmer until they begin to soften. • Add the dulse pieces and the tomatoes [remove skins just before serving] and cook until the dulse is tender and the potatoes begin to break up and thicken the soup.

ALTERNATIVES

Rather than making a soup out of the main ingredients why not bake a simple layer dish? Layers of larger pieces of washed and soaked dulse, sliced potatoes and halved tomatoes. Cover with foil and bake till done.

And consider stir-frying dulse and adding the crispy brown pieces to salad or fish dishes. Also try steaming chopped dulse and serving with sliced apples and a drizzle of olive oil.

KELP & FISH SOUP

6" piece of kelp
1 small onion
1½-2 pints water
1 potato
Fish or shellfish

• Wash the kelp then soak in clean water for 30 minutes. • Meanwhile finely slice the onion and slice the potato thinly. • Cut the fish of your choice into fork sized pieces.

• Cut the soaked kelp into small pieces and simmer in water along with the onion and potato for about 15 minutes - or until almost cooked. • Add the fish, top up with water if necessary and cook until the fish is done.

LAVER CAKES

Purple laver fronds
Water
Oatmeal
Butter or oil

Purple laver seaweed becomes a sort of black-green when cooked and can be made into tasty 'cakes' when mixed with oatmeal. The process of cooking the laver may take 4-5 hours [or even longer] so this is a recipe for those with time on their hands. On the other hand you may just like to buy a packet of prepared laver bread and proceed from that point.

• Wash the laver several times in water. • Chop the fronds, place in a pan and cover with water. • Bring to the boil and then simmer until the laver forms a gelatinous purée which is the basis of the rest of the recipe. • You will need to keep an eye on the water level throughout the cooking and stir occasionally to ensure the laver does not stick to the bottom of the pan.

• Mix the laver mass with medium oatmeal in a proportion of about 4:1, then form into small hamburger-like patties. • Fry in hot butter or oil [in bacon fat is the traditional way], cooking each side for a few minutes.

ALTERNATIVES
Serve the prepared laver with mashed potato or spread on pieces of toast like canapes.

RAZOR SHELL FRIES

Razor clams
Flour or fine meal
Butter
Bacon

You've done the donkey ride, messed yourself up with candyfloss, and done the amusement arcades. Time to find some food... particularly any razor shell clams you manage to extract during low tide.

• Place the razor shells in a pan of cold water. Bring to the boil. • When the shells open remove from the water, separate the meat and set aside.

• Meanwhile fry the bacon in some butter. • Remove the bacon once cooked.
• Take the razor meat and dip in the flour or meal and fry gently in the now quite salty butter. Serve alongside the bacon.

RAZOR SHELL CHOWDER

Razor clam meat	2 or 3 bacon rashers
Butter or oil	1 ½ pints water or fish stock
2 or 3 large potatoes - cubed	Tomato juice or canned tomatoes [optional]
1 large onion - chopped	Cream [optional]

• Fry the bacon in butter or oil until crisp then set aside. • Now fry the chopped onion until it softens then add the cubed potatoes [small sugar lump-sized pieces] and water. • If you use the tomato option reduce the volume of water or fish stock accordingly. And if you want to add any other vegetables do so at this point, but cut them small.

- Cover the pan, bring to the boil then simmer until the potatoes have softened.
- Add the razor shell meat which should also have been diced into small bite-sized pieces. [See previous recipe on how to prepare razor shells.]

ALTERNATIVES
In different circumstances the razor shells could be replaced by salmon cut into chunks - but drop the bacon and tomatoes from the recipe. Part of the water or stock content can be replaced by milk.

SCALLOP POTATO CAKES

Scallops	Dill [optional]
Mashed potatoes	Salt and pepper
1 egg	Flour
Spring onion	Butter or oil

- Chop the spring onion, and dill if you decide to use some, then place in a bowl with the egg, some fairly dry mashed potato and seasoning. • Mix together well. • Flour your hands and pat out the mixture into palm sized cakes then place a scallop in the centre of each and enclose. • Fry for 5 or 6 minutes on each side, or until nicely browned.

ALTERNATIVES
Substitute the potato with another mashed wild rootstock. However, the availability will depend on the coastal hinterland. You could also consider using other sources of fish for similar treatment.

BACON & SCALLOPS

Scallops
Bacon
Spring onion
Cornflour [optional]
Water [optional]

This is a simple way of cooking scallops. • Fry some bacon in a pan until well done. • Remove from the pan. • When cool break the bacon into small pieces. • Meanwhile fry some chopped spring onions, allow to soften ever so slightly then add the scallops to the pan and continue frying for about a minute more [scallops need little cooking]. • Serve and sprinkle the broken bacon pieces over the scallops.

VARIATIONS
For a more oriental twist you can mix up a batter from some cornflour with water or beaten egg, dip the scallops and then fry.

COCKLE PIE

1 pint cooked cockles	1 pint milk
Bacon	½ cup fish stock, water or white wine
1 onion	Salt and pepper
Butter or oil	1 cup fresh breadcrumbs
½ cup flour	1 cup grated cheddar cheese

• Cook the cockles [*see notes on preparing shellfish at the start of the recipes section*].

• Meanwhile, remove the rind from the bacon and chop. • Chop the onion then sauté along with the bacon pieces until the onion softens. • Bit by bit stir in the flour and cook for 1-2 minutes before taking off the heat. • Stir in milk slowly then put back on the heat and, still stirring, bring to the boil. • Cook until the mixture thickens and forms a smooth sauce. • Add the cockles, fish stock and seasoning and cook for another couple of minutes.

• Place the mixture in a shallow ovenproof dish, and sprinkle over the mixed breadcrumbs and grated cheese. • Put under a hot grill until nicely browned. • Best served with potatoes.

GARLIC COCKLE MASH

Potatoes
Onions
Garlic
Butter or oil
Cockles

As with all shellfish you must be careful about where the cockles are harvested from in terms of possible pollution.

• Cook and mash some potatoes. • Meanwhile, chop the onion and garlic finely and sauté in butter until softened and lightly browned. • Add the cockles, a pinch of pepper and cook until done. • Serve on top of portions of mashed potato.

WINKLE SOUP

Winkles
Meal
Butter
Seaweed - carrageen moss
Milk

This is one very much for the seaside. • Boil the winkles in salt water for 5 minutes and remove from their shells [*see page 40*]. • Dust them with a little fine meal then gently fry in some butter.

• Meanwhile boil some carrageen moss seaweed until tender, add a little milk, serve and add the sautéd winkles.

GLOOPY FISH SOUP

1-2 pints fish stock
2-4 bullrush roots
Whole peppercorns
Salt
Finely chopped vegetables [optional]

The verb 'to gloop'. I gloop, he gloops, you gloop... this fish soup gloops too.

The fish stock comes from the head and bones of that pike or other fish you were preparing before and, as there is every chance you are still near the place where those fish were caught, there may be some bullrushes around about to help you make this soup. If there happens to be some fish flesh too, so much the better.

• Peel and parboil the thumb-width bullrush roots, remove from the water and allow to cool so you can handle them. • Cut the roots crosswise as if you were slicing a carrot, so that you end up with pieces about the size of a pound coin.

• Put the sliced roots back in the pan with about ½ pint of the original cooking water, cover, and continue to cook to extract the starch. What we are doing here is trying to emulate the gloopy viscosity of the crab and sweetcorn soup served up in your local Chinese restaurant. • This is also the time to add any finely chopped or shredded vegetables if you want them.

• When the roots have softened enough add the fish stock and a few whole peppercorns. • Continue to heat for another 10-20 minutes, season to taste and serve. • Include the root pieces at your will or you could mash them.

VARIATIONS
Try adding a handful of chickweed two or three minutes before serving. This provides some vegetable greens [chickweed has a very delicate taste which won't adulterate the fish] and adds colour.

Consider, too, a spot of cream mixed in before serving, and the possibility of replacing part or all of the final cooking water with milk. And why not add some flaked fish meat if you have some?

SNAILS

The most common edible snail in Britain is the Garden Snail - *Helix aspersa* - although there is the true Edible Snail - *Helix pomatia* - that was introduced by the Romans while vacationing in Brittanica, but it is rarer.

The problem with snails or, if you prefer to be sniffy, escargots, is that they take ages to prepare and this may not be always practical for the outdoors person. • To begin with you need to starve them of food for several days - the author has even seen it suggested for 8 days. The purpose of this is to clean out possible toxins in the snail's body; commercially raised snails are fed soy-based bran that doesn't impart any distinct flavour to the meat. However, you don't know what your wild snails have been eating hence the precautionary starvation.

• Having starved the snails give them a feed of nettles, lettuce, oat bran or something like that, for a day. • Then wash the snails, sprinkle some salt over to purge, then rinse again in running water until all the slimy gunk has been washed away and the water runs clear. Incidentally, the Romans sometimes fattened their snails on milk.

• You then have two methods of cooking and getting at your snails. In the first case drop them for about 5 minutes in boiling water - which may be seasoned and flavoured with thyme, oregano, bay leaves and basil, for example, or simply be plain water depending on what is ultimately intended with the snails. In any case the snails should start to emerge from their shells as they cook and when nearly done take the pan off the heat, drain the water off, and remove the snails from their shells with the assistance of a skewer or long two-tined fork.

• Trim the head if you feel so inclined, and remove the guts by incising the snail and removing the swollen intestine - the operculum, for those in the know. Rinse again in water.

• A much more sneaky way to make life simple is to put the snails into a pan of cold water with a little salt and leave for a couple of hours for the snails to emerge from their shells. • At that point you turn up heat and start to boil the water. Any shell which fails to produce an emerging snail should be treated as suspect and thrown away.

• There are all sorts of ways you may like to finish and complete the cooking process but the key thing is gentle slow heat, not rapid and harsh heat which will make them tough. Dust your snails with a little meal and gently fry [with or without garlic].... simmer in a butter and wine, or port, sauce.... sauté gently with diced bacon or ham and potatoes [parboil first].... cook in a tomato and onion sauce... or in a more spicy tomato sauce with sliced chorizo sausages.... or even serve them up on garlic toast and topped with a little grated parmesan or the cheese of your choice. Forget putting snails back in their shells, get on with eating them.

FOR YOUR NOTES

VEGGIE THINGS

CHICKWEED RICE BAKE

1 cup chicken stock
1 cup water
Onion
Salt and pepper
Handful fresh chickweed
1 cup of rice
Grated cheese
Butter or oil

'Ahem, what are you doing?' asks a curious onlooker. 'Picking chickweed,' you reply. 'What for?' the inquiring voice continues. 'Why to eat, of course,' says you. 'You're loopy you are.' Well you know better don't you?

• Finely grate or slice a small onion, and sauté until softened. • Mix the rice, onion and chickweed together and place into a small baking dish which has been lightly oiled or greased. • Season, add hot stock and boiling water, and drizzle with a little grated cheese.

• Cover lightly with a piece of foil and bake in a moderate over for 30-40 minutes or until the rice is cooked through. • Remove the foil cover and brown the top.

VARIATION
Lamb's quarters would provide another vegetable alternative to chickweed, but the baking time may need extending by another 5 minutes or so.

FRIED DANDELION FLOWERS

Dandelion* flowers - young
Flour
Butter or oil

• Remove the outer sepals from the young flowers, as these can impart a bitterness to the sweeter young flowers [like the rest of the plant the bitterness increases with age]. • Quickly wash and then shake to remove most of the water. • Coat well in flour and then fry until nicely browned all over - salty butter will provide a savoury counterbalance to the sweeter young flowers.

ALTERNATIVES
Another way of frying up dandelion flowers is to make a batter with flour, baking powder, milk and eggs, then dipping the flowers and frying them until

crisp and brown. Young flowers require no sweetening, but with older and potentially more bitter ones you could make a dip of honey - perhaps spiced to add a piquant edge.

FRIED DANDELION LEAVES

Dandelion* leaves
Oil
Garlic [optional]
Salt

Considering raw green dandelion leaves make the author's toes curl like a pair of Turkish slippers, this is one way of making the leaves more palatable, other than by boiling.

This method of cooking dandelion leaves results in the leaves taking on the same sort of consistency as the so-called 'fried seaweed' that the Chinese prepare.

• If you want to use garlic crush a clove and heat in some oil. • Throw the leaves into the pan and shallow fry until the leaves crispen and take on a dark green appearance. • Remove from the oil, drain, place on absorbant kitchen paper [if possible] and sprinkle lightly with salt. Most, but not all, of the bitterness of the leaves is removed if cooked this way. Discard the tainted oil.

ALTERNATIVES
If you find dandelions bitter in salads or even cooked, you can try counterbalancing the bitterness with orange dressings or apples.

CURRIED DANDELION

Dandelion* leaves
1 garlic clove
Oil
Water
Lime [or lemon] juice
Curry powder [or spices of choice]

Here is a way to hide that bitterness of dandelion yet provide the goodness of the leaves themselves.

• Crush or finely chop a garlic clove, sweat in some oil and then add dandelion leaves and cook gently until wilted. • Add a little water, lemon/lime juice, and curry powder to taste. • Turn up heat and bring to the boil, then cover and gently simmer for about 10 minutes.

VARIATIONS

For simplicity curry powder was used here, but you could try any of the spicy or curry combinations found in the guide as an alternative. And try a combination of dandelion leaves with chopped apples.

VEGETABLE BAKE

1 cup leek
1 cup young salad burnet leaves
1 cup of nettle or dead-nettle leaves
½ cup spring onion
1 tbsp. flour
Salt and pepper
Handful chopped nuts [walnut / hazel / beech masts]
4 eggs
Butter

• Finely chop all the vegetable ingredients and place in a bowl to which is added the flour and seasoning, before mixing thoroughly. • Finally add the nuts.

• Beat the eggs and add them to your vegetables. • Take something like a 5-6″ cake tin and melt the butter in this. • Fill with your mixture. Alternatively you could use something like a small metal handled skillet, quickly seal the bottom of the mixture over the cooker and then bake in the oven. • Cook in a slow preheated oven for 45-50 minutes or until the top is nicely browned.

NETTLE OR FAT-HEN BAKE

Nettles or fat-hen
1 onion
Butter or oil
Eggs
Salt

• Clean, wash and chop leaves. • Place in pan with a dash of salt and sweat till soft.

• Meanwhile, slice and fry a medium sized onion in some oil till soft. • Add the leaves and continue to fry for a couple of minutes, then spread evenly around before breaking a few eggs over the mixture. • Keep heat going for a couple of minutes, before turning off and covering the pan to let the eggs continue cooking. • Can be eaten hot or cold.

FAT-HEN EGGS FLORENTINE

2 pints fat-hen leaves
Nutmeg [optional]
1 tbsp. butter
1 tbsp. flour
1 cup milk
Salt
Cheese - grated
Cayenne
3 or 4 hard-boiled eggs

Spinach-based eggs florentine is one of the old chestnuts, so how about updating it with this adaptation using the leaves of fat-hen which also happen to taste a bit spinach-like and were once grown as a vegetable?

• Cook the washed leaves in their own water for about 5-10 minutes or until tender. • Stir in the butter and pinches of salt and grated nutmeg. • Place this mixture in a greased oven dish and spread evenly.

• In a pan melt some butter and add the flour to make a smooth paste. • Cook for about a minute, making sure to stir. • Add the milk a bit at a time while continuing to stir. • Bring to a gentle boil and cook for a couple of minutes. • Add seasoning, a pinch of cayenne and a handful of grated cheese. • Pour over the fat-hen leaves, sprinkle with some more grated, then slice the hard-boiled eggs and arrange on top. • Bake in a preheated hot oven for about 10 minutes.

NETTLE & CHEESE ROULADE

3-4 pints nettle leaves   Fresh breadcrumbs
½ cup cream   Cheese
3-4 eggs   Pepper
Salt and pepper
Butter and oil

Don't be frightened by the word roulade, just think of a snobby swiss roll. The recipe takes place in several stages, so it is not something to be tackled if you are in a hurry.

To start... • Separate the eggs. • Chop the nettle leaves and wilt with a tiny amount of butter. Continue cooking and stirring until the nettles are almost dry. • Take off the heat and allow to cool down.

• Meanwhile, lightly oil or butter a sheet of kitchen foil and place of a baking tray. • Whisk the egg whites. • Then combine the separated egg yolks [use 4 if small sized], some seasoning and the cream to the cooked nettles, and mix together. • Fold in the beaten egg whites.

• Next... Turn the mixture onto the foil, spread evenly and square-up into a 6 to 8 inch square. • Place in a moderately-hot to hot oven and bake for about 10 minutes, or until firmed up [this will depend on thickness]. • Remove the roulade base, allow to cool then separate from the foil. • Then gently roll the base in the foil to create a naturally curved shape.

• While cooling down make the cheese stuffing mixture with cheese and breadcrumbs. [The cheese is really a matter of personal taste. You can indulge yourself with a lovely stilton, go for a nice gooey mozarella, or simply stick with that old standby, cheddar. Over to you and your tastebuds.] • Grate or crumble the cheese and combine with the breadcrumbs – the breadcrumbs will help reduce oozing of the melting cheese. • Unroll the 'base' and cover with the cheese mixture, then roll up. • To keep the roll 'shaped' you can pin the 'curl' of the roll with twigs whittled down like cocktail sticks, or use real cocktail sticks.

• Place on the baking tray and lightly cover with foil. • Bake in a moderate oven for about 10-15 minutes, or long enough to just melt the cheese. Serve sliced.

ARROWHEAD, FENNEL & STILTON BAKE

Arrowhead roots
Fennel bulb
Stilton
1 small onion
1 garlic clove [optional]
Cream
Vegetable stock
Salt and pepper

This is really a comfort food recipe for those with access to some stilton cheese and cream, and dreaming longingly for comfort food. Dream on!

• Parboil peeled arrowhead tubers and slice when cool enough to handle. • Meanwhile, slice the fennel bulb thinly. • Finely chop the onion. • Place the arrowhead and fennel in the bottom of a baking dish. • Crumble over the stilton, and sprinkle the finely chopped onion on top.

• Mix enough vegetable stock and cream to submerge most of the baking dish ingredients, and season to taste. • Pour over the contents of the dish and bake in a moderate oven till done and nicely browned.

GOOD KING HENRY GRATIN

Good king henry leaves
Butter
Breadcrumbs
Cheese
Salt and pepper

Like chickweed, GKH is available virtually all year round and provides a spinach-like substitute. So here's a way of using it in a gratin.

• Cook the leaves until they just become tender, drain, and then put them into an ovenproof dish which has been greased and dusted with fine breadcrumbs.
• Spread the leaves round evenly, add seasoning and then cover with a mixture of cheese and breadcrumbs. • Add a couple of small pats of butter then bake for 15 minutes in a moderate oven.

NETTLE & SALSIFY GRATIN

2 pints nettle leaves
Salsify roots – cooked [or milk thistle roots]
1 cup stock - vegetable or chicken
1 cup cream
Butter or oil
Salt and pepper

This gratin version drops the cheese element, although you could always add some too.

• Peel the salsify root, chop into 1-inch pieces and parboil in some acidulated water until they begin to tenderize. • Remove from water and drain. • Wilt the nettle leaves in a pan with a little water – just as you would with spinach.
• Spread the vegetables in the bottom of a lightly oiled or greased ovenproof dish and add seasoning. • Put the cream and stock in a pan and heat through while stirring. • Pour over the vegetables and cook in a preheated moderate oven for 30-40 minutes.

VARIATIONS
Something you might like to add are bread croutons which will provide some carbohydrate and a crunchy finish that complements the soft vegetables. These can be sprinkled on when serving, or in the last 10 minutes of cooking. For something even more substantial, fry fingers of bread and lay these on top in the final stages.

RICE WITH DRIED ELDERBERRIES

Rice
Dried elderberries
Hazelnuts / beech masts
2 onions
Cinnamon

• Peel the onions, slice lengthwise and fry. • Finely chop the hazelnuts, or use whole beech masts. • Cook the rice [2 parts water to 1 of rice] letting the water be absorbed rather than boiled off. • Before it is fully cooked add the fried onions, elderberries, nuts and seasoning. • Mix in and finish off cooking.

RICE STUFFED DOCK LEAVES

Dock* leaves	1 cup chopped dill
Olive oil	[or try fennel or wild chervil]
Salt, pepper, cinnamon, allspice	½ cup semi-dried elderberries
2 or 3 finely chopped onions	2½ cups water
1½ cups rice	3 tbsp. lemon juice

This is very similar to a previous stuffed dock leaf recipe with some variations - largely the absence of meat for vegetarians.

• Put 2 or 3 tablespoons of oil in a pan and fry the chopped onions and rice till they take on a light gold appearance.

• Now add the chopped herbs, elderberries and seasoning. • Continue gently frying for 5 minutes then add another slug of oil and 2½ cups of water. • Cover, turn down the heat and simmer until the rice is tender. • Let the mixture cool down before using to stuff your leaves [see *page 58 for method*].

• Put the leaf rolls in the bottom of a pan [lined with extra dock leaves to prevent sticking]. • Pour over the 2 cups of water and the lemon juice. • Cover the pot and cook until tender.

ALTERNATIVES
Try red lentils as a rice substitute. Also try a sweet and sour topping by mixing half a cup each of sugar and vinegar and adding this to the final cooking process. The allspice can be replaced by adding pinches of ground cloves and nutmeg.

For a nutty flavoured rice grate some burdock root [first year's growth], steep in water for 20 minutes and discard the water, and then add to the cooking rice.

ACORN PANCAKES

½ cup fine acorn* mash
½ cup flour
1 tsp. baking powder
Salt - pinch
1 large egg
1 cup milk
1 tbsp. butter
Honey [optional]

By this point most of your friends, neighbours and work colleagues must be truly convinced that you come from another planet. Prove it to them with this little number.

• With the exception of the butter place all the ingredients into a bowl and mix into a smooth batter - a splash of clear honey will add a little sweetness. • Melt the butter and add to the mixture, stirring to evenly distribute. • Pour the mixture into a lightly oiled frying pan. • Cook each side until browned.

ALTERNATIVES
In the absence of flour it is also possible to make a sort of nutty flavoured pancake with the acorn mash, but the egg content needs to be increased to replace the gluten in the flour and help bind the mash. Reduce the amount of milk also, as the mash contains moisture [as much as possible being squeezed out before use].

If you have managed to collect enough pollen from cattails/bullrushes then try replacing the acorn mash component of this recipe with the equivalent of pollen.

ACORN & CHESTNUT FALAFEL

Chestnuts	Salt and pepper
Acorn* mash	Lemon juice
1 onion - grated	Egg
Garlic clove / chopped ramsons	Flour or fine meal
Pinches of ground coriander, cumin,	Oil
and chilli powder	

The inspiration for this is the Greek appetizer. • The acorns should have been leached, cooked, had excess water squeezed out and then been mashed. • The chestnuts will have been boiled till tender, or even baked/roasted, then minced finely - but still having some nutty texture. In both cases the mash needs to be as moisture-free as possible without being a dry flour.

• Combine the chestnut and acorn ingredients in a bowl and add good pinches of the spices, the salt, garlic crushed [or finely chopped ramsons leaves for a milder flavour], the egg beaten, and a slug of lemon juice [but only if this does not make the 'mix' too moist]. • Mix all of this thoroughly together. • Flour your hands and form the mixture into small balls slightly over 1-inch in diameter and then flatten a little. • Dust with the flour or meal and gently fry in a little oil until browned on both sides.

STUFFED ACORN CHAPATI

Acorn meal or mash
Flour
Water

Someone, somewhere, is making a chapati as you read this, and while dry-cooked chapatis produced with acorns are definitely uninspiring - unless served with clear honey or a nice sweet puréed wild fruit like blackberry - stuffing them is another way of bolstering what can only really be regarded as survival food.

Wheat flour is absolutely necessary to provide the gluten content to hold the chapatis together, and should be mixed 2 parts acorn mash to 1 part flour.

• Mix the flour and meal/mash and add a little water at a time to produce a dough that holds, then kneed until smooth [the dough has little elasticity]. • Allow to rest for a while, although you can use straight away. • Take portions of the dough and flatten or roll out to a thickness of about 1/10 th inch and large enough to fit the bottom of a frying pan.

• Take one layer and sprinkle your stuffing mixture over. • Place the second layer on top. • Moisten and crimp the edges [the stuffing should not be too moist] and then place in the bottom of a hot, lightly oiled, frying pan or on a griddle. • Cook for a couple of minutes. • While the first side is cooking lightly brush the top with oil then turn over to cook for another 2-3 minutes.

Since the cooking time is only a few minutes your stuffings need to be to pre-cooked or contain ingredients that do not require cooking. As a stuffing consider mashed wild roots, or wilted leaves mixed with some cream, perhaps even scrambled egg flavoured with spring onion.

ACORN MINI PIZZAS

Acorn meal or mash
Flour
Water
1 tin creamed mushrooms

The idea for this recipe came as a result of observations when working on the acorn chapatis above. And yes, this recipe cheats by using some canned food but it just seems to work as a combination, while mozarella is likely to be in short supply in the wilds. The recipe dispenses with the need for carrying yeast used in traditional pizza dough – but a pinch of baking powder does help!

The pizza base made like this is really quite filling so make them about four or five inches wide and about ¼-inch deep.

• Use the same chapati dough mixture from the previous recipe and briefly cook for a minute on each side in a dry hot frying pan or on a griddle, then remove from the heat. • Cover the base in the topping, place on a metal tray and put in a moderately hot oven for about 10-15 minutes.

VARIATIONS
There is such a wide range of toppings that you could consider from the wild; from creamy vegetarian wild greens to shredded meats and pieces of sliced wild fruit. For readers who like traditional tomato based pizzas why not try a mixture of canned plum tomatoes [drained to remove excess liquid] and slivers of corned beef - items that are likely to be carried in many people's rucksack. Drizzle a little oil over ingredients which have little natural moisture before placing in the oven.

ACORN SEV

Acorn* mash
Potatoes - mashed
Flour
Oil
Salt
Spices [optional]

Sev is a deep-fried extruded snack food from India, and the idea behind this recipe was a version made with wild ingredients which could be added to a trail mix.

One basic problem is that when dropped into lots of hot oil potato and acorn have a tendency to simply dissolve away, hence the need for some flour to help bind things together. However, the mixed 'dough' needs to be soft enough to 'extrude' so it's best to do a small test-run with a few teaspoons of mixture to see how it fries.

• Cook and mash some potatoes, and mix with 'prepared' mashed acorns in a ratio of 1:1 [if you increase the acorn proportion the sev will taste more 'nutty'].
• Then add flour a bit at a time - up to a maximum of a third by volume - so that the dough is soft and pliable rather than firm.

• Next, heat one or two inches of oil in a pan. • When hot extrude the dough into the hot oil - using a piping cone, or if outdoors the method described below. • A knife or a finger can be used to break the dough into manageable pieces before it reaches the pan.

In one instance the author literally used a spare sheet of clean A4 paper twisted into a piping cone. The extrusion hole should be no bigger than ¼-inch wide. Any smaller and the strands tend to burn; wider and the centre does not cook before the outside burns.

• Cook no more than a couple of minutes or until golden brown then remove from the oil.

ALTERNATIVES

In the absence of any flour try mixing the mashed potato and acorn with tomato ketchup so that a quite soft consistency is achieved, then extrude. The author used this with some success when adopting his unconventional A4 paper piping cone.

Untried at the moment - through lack of ingredients - is the thought that mashed sweet chestnuts could substitute for either potatoes or acorn mash.

For a small, more biscuit-like addition to a trail mix, you can mix the main ingredients - or just acorn mash and flour - into a quite firm dough [flavoured if required], roll into a cylinder and then slice into thin wafers which are then deep-fried.

BUCKWHEAT BAKE

2 cups buckwheat
Water
Salt
Butter

From the 16th to 19th centuries buckwheat was a major food staple though it is now grown mainly as a fodder crop and what you will find in the hedgerows are escapees from cultivation. However you can still use the dried seeds [assuming there is enough] make an interesting alternative food to accompany other dishes. In this recipe the buckwheat is simply baked, but you will need to dry the seeds, de-husk and then toast in oil to prepare the buckwheat for cooking [see *Wild Plant Reference section*].

• Put the 'prepared' buckwheat grain into an oven dish and just cover with water. • Sprinkle with some salt and drizzle with butter. • Cover the dish and place in a moderately hot oven for about 15 minutes before reducing to a moderate heat and cooking for a further 2-3 hours.

ALTERNATIVES

Buckwheat can be cooked very slowly to produce a kind of thick porridgy mass. It can be mixed with savoury things like mushrooms or onions, and served with sour cream. You can also mix in ingredients and make fritters to be fried.

NUTTY FRY BREAD

2 cups flour [wild ground flour / ordinary flour]
1-1½ tsp. baking powder
Salt - pinch
1 cup warm milk [or water]
Butter and oil
Hazelnuts or beech masts

This recipe is designed to allow you to experiment with any flours that you have produced from wild plants - acorn, fat-hen, amaranth, or even the starch from bullrushes. These should be mixed in combination with ordinary wheat flour for this recipe.

• Finely chop the hazelnuts or beech masts. • Place all the ingredients except the oil in a bowl and mix thoroughly into a dough. • Roll into a ball, smother the surface with some oil, cover and leave for 30 minutes.

• Take small handfuls of the dough and pat out to about the thickness of a potato cake, then deep-fry in oil or butter.

VARIATIONS

The nut ingredients could be replaced with finely chopped green leaves, or herbs that will quickly cook but not burn in the deep-frying stage. The fry bread could also be served with wild fruit sauces or chutneys. The same dough can also be cooked over an open fire rather than fried.

HOT BULLRUSH FRIES

Bullrush roots
1 Egg
Milk
Salt and pepper
Oatmeal or flour
Mild chilli powder or other spice
Butter or oil

If you *are* going to wade ankle deep in mud to get at some bullrush roots you might as well do something other than merely bake them.

Bullrush roots are fibrous but contain lots of slightly sweetish starch, and this recipe is an attempt to make them a more interesting food source.

• Peel and then boil the bullrush roots until tender. • Drain. • Chop into pieces about 1-2 inches long, or smaller if you prefer. • Beat an egg with a splash of milk and add seasoning and spice. • Dip the bullrush pieces into the egg and then roll in the oatmeal or flour. • Deep-fry the pieces for several minutes, or pan fry in butter until nicely browned.

WILD ROSTI

Waxy potatoes and arrowhead roots
1 small onion [optional]
Wild greens or rootstock, or meat [optional]
Herbs or spices [optional]
Butter or oil

In the world according to Harry Lime the Swiss gave us banking and cuckoo clocks. He missed out the 'rosti'.

Rostis are a simple side dish made from fried shredded potato, and this recipe is left deliberately open-ended in case you have other ingredients that you would like to add the basic potato.

• Coarsely shred some peeled starchy potatoes and arrowhead roots, then squeeze out the excess water [the potatoes may also be parboiled to reduce the remainder of the cooking time]. • If you want to flavour your rosti add a little amount of shredded 'prepared' wild ingredients - like parsnip equivalents such as caraway or sweet cicely roots, or incorporate some wild greens.

• Put some butter or oil in a pan [non-stick preferred] and heat until it is very hot. • Swirl around the pan bottom, then spread the grated ingredients evenly across the bottom. • Press down with the back of a spoon or a slice until firm. • Turn down the heat to medium and cook for about ten minutes - or until the bottom begins to crispen [a process a bit like the RABBIT HASH BROWN recipe]. • Slide the rosti out of the pan onto a plate then invert it with the aid of another plate. • Meanwhile add more butter or oil to the frying pan and heat. • When bubbling slip the rosti back to cook the other side. • About 10-15 minutes, depending on thickness. • Cut into portions and serve.

VARIATIONS
As this is a dish cooked with lots of fat why not serve it with some healthy wilted wild greens, some sour cream or even a variation of a white sauce? On the other hand you might just opt for a sprinkling of fried bacon.

SALAD BURNET YOGHURT

1-2 cups of fresh plain yoghurt
1 cup young salad burnet leaves
1 tbsp. fresh dill
Salt and pepper

In the Middle East cucumber yoghurt is commonly served as either an accompaniment to a dish or as salad appetiser in its own right. Hence this unusual variant which could accompany something spicy - perhaps the spicy bullrush fries mentioned previously.

• The burnet leaves - which taste a bit like cucumber - need to be very young and chopped finely before being mixed with the yoghurt, adding seasoning to taste. Older burnet leaves become tough and are really only fit to be cooked.

NETTLE ALOO

Nettles	1-2 garlic cloves
Potatoes	1 tsp. ground coriander and paprika
Water	Pinches of ground cardamom seed & cayenne
Butter or oil	Ground black pepper
Mustard seeds	Salt
1 large onion - sliced	

Sag Aloo is one of those wonderful Indian side dishes and this version uses the spinach-like common nettle as a replacement. Roll on nettle aloo...

• Cut the potatoes into 1-inch sized pieces and place into a pot with the nettle leaves. • Cover with some warm water, bring to a rapid boil then simmer for 10-12 minutes, or until the potato pieces are tender.

• In another pan heat butter or oil and cook the mustard seeds until they start to pop. • Add onion sliced lengthways and garlic, and sauté till softened, then add the spices. • Stir around then remove from the heat to add the drained potato and nettles. • Stir everything together gently so the potatoes don't disintegrate, and add any seasoning at this stage. • Continue simmering gently until the whole mass has lost more water.

VARIATIONS
There are other wild ingredients that might make for interesting variations on this recipe. Some of the larger rootstocks for example, and perhaps leaves like borage, ground-elder [pre-cooked to remove the bitter edge], or elder flowers. Chickweed comes to mind too, although it is so delicate that you would have to add it later in the cooking process to prevent it becoming a green sludge.

WILDERNESS VEGETABLE KURMA

2 cups wild vegetables [ie. alexanders, milk thistle, burdock]
1 small onion
Butter or oil
1 chilli [optional]
Garlic clove
Coriander and cinnamon - larger pinches
Turmeric and ginger - smaller pinches
Cardamom pod
Cloves - or grated herb bennett
1 cup water
Coconut cream
Salt - pinch

Bring a touch of the local curry house to your corner of the wilderness...

There are lots of variables in this recipe, given that you may only have some of ingredients to hand and, in truth, to be a real kurma coconut is a must - but you decide. Adapt and play with this at your pleasure, while the basic ingredient list is a roughly for preparing a single portion.

• Chop a variety of wild rootstock and stems, and also a medium sized onion.

• Gently fry pinches of cinnamon, a couple of cloves and a cardamom pod in some oil or butter for a couple of minutes [in a deep pan if cooking for several people]. • Next add the chopped onion, and a de-seeded chilli. • Continue frying until the onion starts to brown. • Then add a crushed garlic clove [or less if you prefer] and a pinch of ginger and continue gently frying for another minute of so. • Tip the chopped vegetables into the pan and cook for another couple of minutes.

• Then add the water, a pinch of turmeric and briefly bring to the boil before reducing the heat to a very gentle simmer [this is a long slow cook recipe]. • As the vegetables begin to tender add some coconut cream and a pinch of salt, and cook until the vegetables are tender.

WILD ROOTS & STEM CURRY

2-3 pints of mixed roots and stems
Butter or oil
Salt
½ tsp. each of mustard seeds & cayenne
1 tsp. each of turmeric, ground coriander & cumin seeds
2 cups water
1 carton plain yoghurt

This is really an opportunity to make a vegetable curry from selected rootstocks and substantial stemmed wild plants. If you have access to the individual spices then you can tinker with the flavours, otherwise you might just want to reach for a sachet of curry powder.

• It's best to pre-cook the individual vegetables since many will have different preparation requirements, and then dice them. • Once you've accomplished that put the spices into some heated oil and simmer for a couple of minutes, adding a good pinch of salt.

• Add the diced vegetables, stir to make sure everything is coated in the curry and cook until crisp-ish. • Add the water and simmer gently for 15-20 minutes giving the occasional stir. • Stir in the yoghurt and leave to heat through for a few more minutes. Serve.

CURRIED WILD VEGETABLES

Butter or oil
Wild greens / vegetables
1 tsp. mustard seed
Cumin seeds, chilli and turmeric powder - pinches
Salt

Faster than a streak of lightning in your local take-away, this is a method of nicely currying wild greens and vegetables.

• Variously chop and slice wilderness greens and vegetables. • Very briefly fry mustard and cumin seeds and chilli in oil or butter. • Add the vegetables to the spices, along with a pinch of turmeric and salt to taste. • Raise the heat for a few minutes, cover and then cook very gently at a low heat until cooked.

CAJUN BLACKBERRIES & HAZELNUT COUSCOUS

Blackberries
Butter or oil
1 small onion or shallot
Paprika, cayenne, cumin, black pepper, mustard powder
Oregano and thyme
Water
Hazelnuts - chopped
Couscous

• Finely chop the onion or shallot and sauté in a little oil until soft. • Mix pinches of the spices and herbs together and add to the pan, stirring over the heat for a few minutes so that the flavours are released. • Add blackberries to the pan with a knob of butter, a splash of water and a pinch of salt. • Heat until the blackberries begin to soften but don't disintegrate, then remove from the heat but keep warm.

• Meanwhile, place the dried couscous in a dish and add boiling water. • Allow to rise and absorb water before mixing in the chopped hazelnuts. • Serve and spoon the spiced blackberries over.

VARIATIONS
In the absence of the range of spices needed for cajun style flavouring you may just like to use straight curry powder, cayenne, or even no spices at all and keep the dish as a sort of vegetarian fruit one. If the blackberries are too sweet a little lemon or splash of cider vinegar can be used to take the edge off the sweetness. Apply the cajun spice mix to game meat too.

WILD COUNTRY CROQUETTES

Potatoes
Shepherd's purse leaves [or other wild greens]
Milk
Butter and oil
Flour
Salt and pepper
Hazelnuts - handful
Eggs
Breadcrumbs

• Cook and mash some potatoes. • Also boil the shepherd's purse leaves until tender, chop the hazelnuts and, if using fresh breadcrumbs, use the time to dry them. • Drain the wild greens and chop finely.

• In a pan melt some butter and stir in a little flour while cooking gently for a couple of minutes until the mixture thickens. • Add a spot of milk to thin and then blend in the chopped shepherd's purse leaves. • More milk may be added to provide extra liquid but don't make too wet. • Raise the heat to bring the mixture to the boil then simmer for a few minutes. • Add the mashed potato, hazelnuts and seasoning then mix thoroughly.

• Allow the mixture to cool and firm up - preferably briefly chill - then roll into croquettes. • Dip in beaten egg and breadcrumbs then deep-fry in oil until crisp and nicely browned. • Remove from the oil, drain and serve.

VARIATIONS
The contents of these croquettes could contain all sort of ingredients, and even be spiced if that is your preference. As an accompaniment why not try a sweet dip of some sort for dunking your croquettes like a Chinese spring roll?

SPRING GREENS POTATO ROLL

Mashed potato
Milk
Wild spring leaves [nettles, ground ivy, caraway]
Butter or oil
Eggs
Salt and pepper
Water

• Mash cooked potatoes and some milk then add a couple of beaten eggs, a good chunk of butter and seasoning. • Combine together to form an even mixture. • Put the mixture onto a dampened piece of cloth [a clean tea towel will do] and flatten out. A ½ to ¾-inch depth will suffice.

• Chop the spring vegetable leaves, gently fry in some butter, and then spread across the flattened potato mash. • Using the cloth to catch the end of the potato begin rolling the 'roll'. • Place this in a baking tray the bottom of which has been greased with butter, or oiled. • Give a quick brush with milk and bake for about half an hour. • Can be served with a dollop of sour cream.

VARIATIONS
This idea of a 'roll' could be applied to other sorts of mashed wild rootstocks and incorporating either sweet or savoury fillings. Also chestnuts would be an interesting candidate for experimenting with.

CHESTNUT & SALSIFY CROQUETTES

2 cups salsify - cooked
2 cups chestnuts - cooked
2 eggs
Ground coriander or chilli – pinches [optional]
2 slices white bread - crumbed
Butter and oil
Salt and pepper

This is a recipe for using those preserved sweet chestnuts that you've squirreled away [or frozen if you happen have a deep freeze for long-term storage].

• Boil peeled, chopped salsify root for about 20-30 minutes in lightly acidulated water [this prevents the salsify from becoming discoloured] or until tender, then drain and mash with a fork. • Similarly, roughly mash 2 cups of cooked sweet chestnuts. • Place the two mashes in a bowl with 1 egg yolk, some seasoning, and the spice ingredients if you wish. • Mix together well.

• Beat the second egg. • Form the mixture into croquettes then dip in beaten egg, roll in breadcrumbs, and fry in a small amount of oil. • Keep turning the croquettes so that they are nicely browned all over.

WILD STUFFED POTATOES

Small-medium size potatoes
Butter or oil
Lady's Smock [young leaves / flower heads] or young dandelion flowers
Salt and pepper

• Select potatoes that are about 1½-2 inches in diameter, peel, and then hollow out a cavity. The cored potato can be saved and used in soup or for another recipe which calls for potato. • Fry, trying to get as much all round browning as possible.

Meanwhile to prepare the vegetable stuffing... • Strip the bittercress leaves from their stalks and sweat in some butter until they begin to soften. • Stuff the potatoes, and place in a baking dish. • Dribble a bit of oil or smear with a dab of butter, and then cook in a moderate oven for about 10 minutes, or until the potatoes are cooked through. • In the absence of an oven the potatoes may also be lightly wrapped in foil and cooked on the embers of a campfire.

ALTERNATIVES

The filling for the potatoes can also be extended to meat and fish, adding whatever herbs and spices are at hand, and also smearing the potatoes with tomato purée before popping in the oven.

Alternative wild greens could be used, such as sow-thistle leaves with some butter, cream and seasoning - and dropping the tomato purée as an ingredient. On the other hand, why not try a sweet filling of blackberries, suitably spiced up? Or try a combination of apple with dandelion leaves given one boiling.

WILD NEEPS n TATTIES

Arrowhead roots - or potatoes
Sweet cicely roots - or turnips
Salt
Butter
Milk

Well almost! Real Neeps and Tatties can never truly be replaced but this recipe was inspired by the spirit of that famous Scots dish. Unfortunately there are really no decent wild turnip-like equivalents for cultivated turnips and other root stocks have to substitute. In this case those of aniseedy sweet cicely. You may want to peel the arrowhead tubers as the skin imparts a very slight bitterness.

The proportion of potato to turnip ingredients is traditionally 2:1, but since arrowhead tubers are small you may like to play with the proportions.

• Slice the peeled arrowhead roots or potatoes and place in a pan with just enough water to cover. • Bring to the boil, cover, and then simmer until the potatoes are tender.

• Meanwhile dice the sweet cicely roots into pieces the size of a sugar cube, then place in another pan with a good pinch of salt, and enough water to cover. • Again, bring to the boil, cover and simmer until tender.

• Drain the arrowhead roots or potatoes and mash till no lumps remain - a low speed blend will accomplish the same if you happen to be doing this at home. • Add a pinch of salt, 2 tablespoons of melted butter, and a little warmed milk. • Blend together until smooth. • Then add some more milk and whisk in to fluff up the mixture.

• Drain the sweet cicely roots, place back in the pan and drizzle over some melted butter and toss. • Serve with your tatties.

HERB DUMPLINGS

1 cup flour
1 tsp. baking powder
Salt and pepper
Herbs
1 egg
½ cup milk
Stock [optional use]

Remember those dreadful dumplings served up at school? The ones the Romans used to breach the walls of cities under siege? Well this recipe offers a much tastier addition for the meat dishes in this guide. The choice of herb is really in your hands, but a suggestion [apart from the fact they are available] is that you choose ones which go well with the particular meat. Check the *Quick Reference Herb Guide*.

• Combine the flour, baking powder and seasoning in a bowl making sure that everything is well mixed and there is no lumpiness in the flour. • Finely chop the herbs of choice and mix with the flour. • In another dish beat ½ cup of milk and the egg. • Add this to the flour mixture and stir in, adding more milk if necessary to produce a dough which is not runny but equally not too firm.

- Spoon the dough into gently boiling water - stock is preferable - cover, and cook for about 15 minutes.

ALTERNATIVES
Replace up to a half of the flour component with fine acorn mash or flour.

SORREL OMELETTE

Sorrel* leaves - finely chopped
Eggs
Butter

The making of an omelette hardly requires description so... • For a sorrel omelette add the chopped leaves just before the omelette is folded over. They will wilt with the heat and provide a piquant edge.

ALTERNATIVES
For something gentle and fragrant add a handful or two of primrose* flowers to your omelette. Speaking of primrose flowers, back in the 15th/16th century they would make primrose pudding. If you wish to experiment, try modifying the HAZELNUT PUDDING recipe [*page 161*].

BORAGE & MINT SALSA

Borage leaves
Mint leaves
Oil
Vinegar
Salt and pepper

You tango. Me salsa!... A salsa is mostly associated with something hot and peppery, yet strictly speaking a salsa is simply chopped vegetable with some addition of oil and vinegar. This recipe draws on the wider interpretation and uses borage as a flavouring alternative to cucumber.

Use young borage leaves [they get more hairy with age] and include some of the small leaf stems to add more texture. • Simply fine chop the borage and mint. • Place in a dish. • Add oil and vinegar and seasoning and mix through. Serve as an accompaniment.

ALTERNATIVES
Walnuts and chives could go well with the mixture too. And why not make a cooling yoghurt side dish by incorporating the borage and/or mint into plain yoghurt?

CREAMED SWEET CICELY

Sweet cicely roots
Cream
Salt and pepper

A very simple way to provide a tasty vegetable mash to accompany a meat dish.

• Peel the roots, chop into pieces and then boil until they are tender enough to mash. • Drain off the water. • If a purée-like consistency is preferred use a hand blender, otherwise mash with a fork or potato masher in the pan. • Stir in enough single cream to provide the preferred consistency, add a little seasoning and gently heat [this prevents the cream curdling], stirring to ensure the mash is evenly mixed with the cream and warmed through.

HONEYED SWEET CICELY

Sweet cicely roots
Butter or oil
Honey

• Peel the roots and then sauté until generally browned all over. • Place on a roasting tray [you could also cover and bake the roots too] and place in a pre-heated hot oven. • Roast for 15-20 minutes and turn the pieces from time to time. • Then dribble over some clear honey and ensure that they are fully covered. • Return to the oven and cook for another 5-10 minutes or until done. • Dribble the remaining honey in the tray over the served roots.

BAKED ALEXANDERS IN CREAM

Alexanders stem
Allspice - pinch
Garlic clove
Cream
Breadcrumbs

Alexanders are best in spring and this is a method of using their celery-like stems, although you may like to extend the recipe to other similar wild ingredients.

• Strip away extraneous side shoots and peel off the outer skin. • Cut the stems into manageable lengths and blanche in boiling water for 2-3 minutes then drain. • Place in an ovenproof dish.

• Crush the garlic clove and combine with a cup of single cream and a pinch of allspice [or alternatives below]. • Pour this over the stems and then sprinkle with breadcrumbs. • Place in a moderately hot oven and bake for about an hour or until the stems are tender.

ALTERNATIVES

The allspice can be replaced by the equivalent of mixed ground cloves, cinnamon and nutmeg. For anyone limited to a campfire, you could slowly bake the alexanders in foil with the crushed garlic, allspice and a little oil then, when cooked, add cream to the juices left behind in the foil and pour over when serving.

BURDOCK IN MUSTARD SAUCE

Burdock flower stems
1 small onion
Butter or oil
1 tbsp. flour
½ pint milk
2 tsp. mustard
Cheese
Salt and pepper

• Use pre-flowering stems [year 2 growth], trim off side shoots and flower bud cluster, and peel outer skin. • Cut into 1-2 inch lengths [think of the size of rhubarb in a pie or crumble] and tenderize in boiling water - about 10 minutes or more depending on stem thickness. • Drain, put in a dish and keep warm.

• Meanwhile, grate the cheese. • Chop the onion finely and sauté until soft and beginning to brown. • Stir in the flour and cook for about a minute before adding the milk a bit at a time while stirring. • Raise heat, bring to the boil and cook for several minutes continuing to stir. • Add the grated cheese, the mustard [exact amount may depend on your preference], and seasoning. • Cook gently for several more minutes keeping stirring. • Pour over the burdock stems and serve.

ALTERNATIVES

Try serving tenderized burdock stems with a sauce made with a chicken stock base and yoghurt and sour cream added. And perhaps sprinkle over some chopped fried bacon.

Alternatively, try an Italian approach with canned tomatoes, onion, garlic and herbs... and even sprinkle grated parmesan over. Or even a creamy sauce sprinkled with breadcrumbs and browned under the grill.

SOW-THISTLE À LA CRÊME

Sow-thistle or milk thistle leaves
1 tsp. salt
2 tbsp. butter
2 tbsp. flour
½ cup cream
Water

This is one way that you might tackle the rather unappealing looking sow-thistle or milk thistles, the leaves of both being edible despite their fierce appearance.

• Cut off the outer spiny edge then drop the leaves into some salted boiling water, cooking till softened. • Over a low heat melt the butter and flour, and mix together. • Add the cream and stir in well, and a couple of tablespoons of water [even milk] to thin further. • Continue cooking just at the boil for about 10 minutes then add the tenderized leaves. • Turn the heat down and simmer for a few more minutes.

ALTERNATIVES
The same cream sauce base could be used with the stems of alexanders, wild angelica*, burdock and even true thistles once they have been boiled till tender. One thought - so far untried through limited stocks of sow-thistles - was that it might be interesting to replace the cream in the recipe with coconut cream and try different spice combinations to give the dish a curry-like edge. Over to you.

POTATOES SIMMERED IN SAUCE

Boiled potatoes - or arrowhead / sweet cicely roots
Butter
Flour
1 cup water [stock preferably]
1 cup milk
Salt
Handful herbs

The boiled potatoes here could be substituted by other starchy edible rootstocks like arrowhead, or parsnip-like roots of sweet cicely, while the recipe offers an additional way of cooking these.

• Once cooled, slice the potatoes. • In a pan melt about two tablespoons of butter, the same amount of flour, then add the water, milk, a pinch of salt and stir and simmer for about 10 minutes, making sure to continue stirring so that a smooth sauce develops. • Add another large knob of butter and a handful of the herb of your choice. • Stir this in and let the herb taste diffuse into the sauce for a couple of minutes. • Add the sliced potatoes and keep heated gently for a few more minutes.

The herb used could be parsley, fennel leaves, sweet cicely, or something peppery such as bittercress or cuckooflower.

THISTLES IN ORANGE

Thistle* stalks
Orange juice
Butter or oil
Salt and pepper

More strange looks from over the fence as you pick your thistles...

• Peel 'young' thistle stalks, and then par-boil for a few minutes in slightly acidulated water [the acidulation prevents discolouration]. • Remove from the water and place in an oven dish which has been lightly oiled on the bottom, add seasoning, a knob of butter, and the juice of an orange. • Cover with foil and bake in a pre-heated hot oven for about 10-15 minutes, or until nice and tender. • This can also be adapted to campfire cooking with the last stage carried out with the stalks parcelled in foil and then placed over hot embers.

ALTERNATIVES
Another way you might like to deal with thistles is to curry them; either on their own or as a contributory ingredient. See the WILDERNESS VEGETABLE KURMA recipe for details.

SIMMERED ORIENTAL KNOTWEED

Japanese knotweed stalks - young
Sesame oil
Soy sauce
Garlic cloves
Chilli - pinch

Ever wondered what to do with that persistent weed? Use about a 1-1 ½ cups of the young lemony flavoured stalks per person.

• Place some sesame oil - this is preferred over other types for this dish - in a heavy bottomed pan, then add a slug of soy sauce, crushed garlic and some chilli powder. • Raise the heat and cook gently for a few minutes. • Add the knotweed stalks and toss to ensure the fronds are covered with the mixture. • Cover and cook over a low heat until the stems are tender - generally 15-20 minutes. Add a splash of water if things look to be getting a bit dry.

WILDERNESS PAKORAS

Flour
Warm water
Cayenne pepper, garam masala, paprika
Salt
Wild vegetables
Oil

Pakoras are a savoury vegetable fritter and the idea for this recipe came after a visit to the Weald Wood Fair. Normally pakoras use chick pea flour as an ingredient for the batter, but in the absence of that ordinary flour will suffice - although you may like to experiment with other wild food flours. Also, you might prefer to use other spicy alternatives - cinnamon, cloves and ginger. Over to you on that account.

• Put some flour in a bowl and gradually stir in water until a thick batter forms.
• Add pinches of the spices and salt, and beat into the batter.

• Meanwhile prepare your wilderness greens and vegetables of choice and slice or keep whole as required. • Leaves can be dipped whole in the batter, stems chopped, and rootstocks sliced [in some cases these will need to be 'prepared' and pre-cooked ready for use].

• Deep fry the battered vegetables until golden brown. • Depending on the hotness you prefer, perhaps serve with a sweet clear honey sauce.

BUTTERED WILD GREENS

Leaves of fat-hen, nettle, burnet, rape, mustard, ground elder
Butter
Salt and pepper
Bread
Oil

This is inspired by a very old English recipe which demanded copious amounts of clarified butter, but it is one easily adapted to anyone cooking in the wild.

The selection of greens is ultimately what you can find locally, but the idea is to have a variety of types and textures. However, avoid using bitter leaves that require a couple of boilings [or pre-boil such leaves], and watch the amount of mustard leaves.

• Remove the stalk material then chop the leaves roughly. • Place in a pan, just cover with water and add a large chunk of butter. • Cover, bring to the boil, then simmer until tender. In an ideal world there will not be much water left in the pan. • Depending on how salty the butter is add seasoning and stir through.

• Meanwhile, dice some old bread and fry in a little oil until golden brown.
• Serve these sprinkled over the dished greens.

BURDOCK ROOT CRISPS

Burdock root – shredded
Breadcrumbs or meal
Flour
Egg
Cayenne, paprika and ground cumin – pinches
Salt and pepper
Oil

• Shred the burdock root diagonally to create a larger surface area and with about $1/10^{th}$ inch thickness. • Drop into plenty of simmering water and cook until the pieces start to soften. • Remove from the heat, drain and plunge into cold water and allow to soak for 10-15 minutes [this allows more of the bitterness to be drawn out without cooking the pieces of root].

• Meanwhile, beat an egg. • To the fine breadcrumbs or meal, and about a tablespoon of flour, add pinches of the spices and some seasoning. • Drain the burdock and pat dry. • Heat some oil in a pan for deep frying. • Dip the pieces of root in the egg and then dunk in the savoury breadcrumb mixture. • Carefully drop into the hot oil and fry for several minutes until the coating is nice and crisp. • Remove from the oil and drain. • Depending on your preferences, serve with a sweet dip – honey and a puréed fruit, for example.

SHEPHERD'S PURSE & JUNIPER BERRIES

1 small onion
1 garlic clove
Juniper* berries
Butter or oil
Shepherd's purse leaves / young shoots

• Chop the onion finely and sweat until soft in some butter or oil, along with a crushed garlic clove and a pinch of lightly crushed juniper berries. • Stir in the shepherd's purse leaves and mix thoroughly to distribute. • Cover the pan and cook over a low heat until the leaves are wilted but not too soft.

CRAB-APPLE CHEESE CASSEROLE

1-1½ pints crab-apples
Butter or oil
Sugar [optional]
1 egg
Milk
1½ cups grated cheese
1 cup breadcrumbs
Salt and pepper

Don't get crabby, get even... And give your pork or ham a lift with this accompaniment.

• Halve the crab-apples lengthwise, remove the core material then slice lengthways again. • Warm in a small pan with a little butter until they just begin to soften, and check for taste to see how tart they are. • Add a little sugar to correct the sharpness if necessary.

• Meanwhile, beat an egg with about a cup of milk and add some seasoning. • Remove the apples from the heat and spread in the bottom of a shallow oven dish, and pour the egg and milk over them. If necessary add a bit more milk to nearly submerge the apples. • Place in a moderate oven for 25-30 minutes or until the apples begin to get tender. • Sprinkle the top with the grated cheese and then the breadcrumbs and return to the oven until the cheese is melted; though a flash under the grille will speed things up.

VARIATIONS
Sliced cooking apples can be used instead of the crab-apples, and you might like to experiment with different types of cheese ranging from the sharp to the mild cheddars.

COUNTRY CHEESE SALAD

Wild purslane - young leaves [or chosen alternative]
1 small onion
1 hard-boiled egg, sliced
Handful chickweed
¼ cup cheddar cheese, diced into small bits
Lemon juice
Mayonnaise [optional]
Garlic [optional]
Salt

• Hard-boil an egg and slice. • Cube some cheddar cheese [or something else of your choice]. • Slice the onion very finely. • Roughly chop the chickweed and young purslane leaves. • Mix the ingredients together in a bowl, drizzle over a bit of lemon juice and season with salt. Mix and serve.

BURDOCK SALAD

Burdock root - sliced and cooked
Spring onion
Eggs – hard-boiled
Horseradish - creamed
Mustard powder
Mayonnaise
Cream or sour cream [optional]
Salt and pepper

• Cook the roots [see *Plant Reference Section*] and slice. • Meanwhile, prepare hard-boiled eggs and slice the spring onion. • Quarter the eggs when cooled.

• In a bowl mix a small amount of creamed horseradish and a pinch of mustard powder then add mayonnaise to increase the volume of the dressing. Cream or sour cream can be used to thin, extend or replace the mayonnaise. • Stir in the spring onions, thinly sliced burdock roots and seasoning to taste. • Serve with the quartered eggs on top.

VARIATIONS
For more greenery in the salad add pieces of burdock stem - suitably cooked and prepared. Or simply add another of your favourite wild salad greens.

WATERCRESS SALAD

Watercress*
Cider vinegar
Honey
Oil
Spring onion [optional]

Remembering the safety cautions that apply to the use of wild watercress this is one way of preparing something salady with the peppery greens, and complementing their taste with a sweet dressing.

• Wash the leaves very well and pick out the tenderest sprigs. • Very finely slice the spring onion lengthwise. • In a bowl mix cider and honey in a proportion of 3:2, then add a slug of a good quality oil. • Add the greens to the dressing and toss.

WOULD-BE RADISH SALAD

Nipplewort leaves - young
Mint leaves
Lemon and orange juice
Salt

For the 'would-be' in many of us, here's another one...

Use about ½ cup of the radish flavoured nipplewort leaves and a couple of mint leaves per person.

• Put some finely chopped the mint leaves in a bowl. • Add a small pinch of salt and freshly squeezed lemon and orange juice [vary the ratio to your preference for sweet or sour]. • Add the trimmed leaf greens and toss to distribute the dressing.

HOP SALAD

Hop shoots - young
Butter and oil
Vinegar
Parmesan [optional - but good]

Two different ways to tackle a hop salad here - one hot and one cold.

• Steam, or boil the young hop shoots for about 10 minutes, until done. • Serve hot with a bit of melted butter drizzled over and a few shavings of parmesan. • Serve cold with a vinaigrette dressing [or even with mayonnaise].

ROSE HIP SOUP

Rose hips
Water
Cornflour

Rose has some great looking hips on her...

This soup may not be to your liking but it is worth experimenting with, not least because rose hips are high in vitamin C. [Check the palatability of the hips before you begin the recipe.] Use only the best blemish free and plump hips you can find.

• Remove the beards and stems, and then cook in their own volume of water.
• When soft, take off the heat, mash and sieve. • Add more water and simmer,

adding some cornflour mixed with water to thicken the soup which can be eaten hot or cold.

ALTERNATIVES
There's the possibility of a sweet and sour version by adding sugar and vinegar to the cooking process. And you might like to experiment with small additions of some of your favourite spices.

GOOD KING HENRY SOUP

1-2 pints good king henry leaves
1 ½ pints chicken or vegetable stock
Lemon juice
Salt and pepper

• Chop the leaves and put into a pan with the stock, a splash of lemon juice, and some seasoning. • Bring to the boil and simmer till tender. • Strain off the liquor and mash the leaves through the sieve. If you happen to have a blender employ that to purée the leaves - it saves personal energy. • Put everything back on the heat and simmer for a few more minutes. • Serve with some lightly fried croutons.

CURRIED CARAWAY ROOT SOUP

1 pint caraway roots
Butter and oil
1 large onion
Cayenne, ground coriander, cumin and turmeric
Salt
Garlic
Flour
2 pints of vegetable stock
Cream

It is sometimes claimed that the roots of the caraway taste better than parsnips themselves, so it seemed like a good idea to do something exotic here.

• Boil the caraway roots until they are very tender, drain off the water and slice. • Meanwhile in another pan sweat a chopped onion in butter or oil along with the spices and salt, then add in a several good pinches of flour for thickening. • Cook for another couple of minutes, stirring the mixture. • Add the stock and sliced caraway roots and cook for another 10 minutes or so.

You now have two options... Serve the soup as it is or, if you are at home, run it through a blender adding some cream. Outdoors you might consider mashing the roots with a fork before the final cooking stage if you wanted a roughish textured soup.

VARIATION
As an alternative to caraway root try the roots of sweet cicely which have a slight aniseedy-liquorice flavour. You may also like to add some chopped wild greens of choice, suitably prepared.

CHICKEN & CHICKWEED SOUP

Chickweed
1 pint chicken [or other] stock
Flour or cornflour [optional]
Cream

Yes, it's time to embarrass the locals again and go a-gathering chickweed. What must they think of you by now?

• Since chickweed has a delicate flavour and also requires very little cooking, place in a pan with a small knob of butter and wilt the leaves - which will take about 2 minutes. You will need several good handfuls of the greens as chickweed shrinks in volume when cooked.

• In a separate pan place the stock. • Bring to the boil then turn down the heat. • Add the wilted chickweed [or just add the leaves raw] and stir in a good dollop of cream. Serve.

• For a thicker soup add the thickening agent to the stock before you bring it to the boil, and maintain the heat until it has cooked before combining with the chickweed.

VARIATIONS
Chicken stock could be replaced by stock made from any other meat leftovers and bones recently prepared. For a more spicy alternative to the chicken soup try seasoning with a little ginger, nutmeg, paprika or turmeric.

DRIED NETTLE & BEEF STOCK SOUP

Dried nettle leaves
1 pint beef stock
Flour or cornflour

Dried common nettle or dead nettle leaves are actually very fragile and can easily disintegrate, but the advantage of these ingredients is that the dried leaves and stock cubes weigh very little and are therefore easy to carry.

• In a pan dissolve a beef stock cube in a pint of water and then add the dried nettles. • Give a quick stir to disperse the dried nettle leaves and let these re-hydrate for 5 minutes. • Turn the heat up and boil for around 5 minutes or until tender. • Add pepper to taste - since the stock may well be salty.

VARIATIONS
If you like your soups thicker then add a bit of thickening. Obviously you could use beef extract instead of stock cubes. The addition of some spices complementary to the beef may be interesting - ginger, coriander, chilli, cloves.

ARROWHEAD & WATERCRESS SOUP

1 pint arrowhead tubers
Watercress*
Butter
½ cup milk
1 pint water
Salt and pepper

Arrowhead tubers, which are about walnut size, taste potato-like so this soup draws upon this. For larger quantities you may need to add or substitute potatoes if arrowhead tubers are in short supply.

• Clean the tubers, peel and boil till tender, remove from the water and push through a sieve, or grate. • Chop a handful of watercress [check *Wild Plant Reference section*], and gently soften in a pan with a knob of butter. • Stir in the milk then add the water, season and simmer for a few minutes.

SORREL SOUP

2 handfuls sorrel* leaves
1 potato
Butter
1-2 pints stock
Sugar

Henry VIII apparently had a penchant for sorrel. Perhaps its sharp taste was responsible for those irritable moments of his.

• Chop the sorrel leaves, and the peeled potato into small pieces. • Fry the potato in a little butter in a deep pan. • Add the stock and cook for 10-15 minutes, then drop in the chopped sorrel leaves and a good pinch of sugar to counteract the tanginess. • Stir and cook for another few minutes but don't cook too long as sorrel takes on a rather unappealing camouflage green colour.

SPRING LEAF SOUP

2-3 pints water or stock
Flour
Butter
2-3 handfuls of chopped mixed leaves
[ie. nettles, ground ivy, caraway]
Salt and pepper
1 egg yolk

• Begin by making a roux [see *CRAYFISH GUMBO recipe on page 101*] then add the water or stock. • Boil for around 10 minutes then add your chosen chopped spring leaves plus some seasoning. • Bring to the boil and whisk in the egg yolk.

SPRING LEAF SOUP - 2

Leaves of yarrow*, sorrel*, dandelion* & nettle
1 small onion
1 garlic clove, chopped
Flour
Butter or oil
2 pints water
2 cups milk
1 egg
Salt and pepper

Here's a more extensive variation on the above using tender early spring leaves. You will need to amend leaf preparation depending on whether you have a blender available or not.

• Boil the water and add the spring leaves [whole if using a blender, or finely chopped if not]. • Add seasoning, cover and simmer for 5-10 minutes. Use about ½-1 cup of each of the leaf types - ½ cup in the case of yarrow as it is peppery. If using dandelion leaves you may prefer to pre-boil the leaves so their bitterness doesn't taint the soup.

• Remove from the heat, strain the cooking water off [but keep], and then purée the leaves in a blender with some milk. • If a blender is unavailable force the leaves through a sieve or crush with the back of a wooden spoon.

• Fry the chopped onion in some butter or oil until they soften and brown, then stir in about a tablespoon of flour and keep stirring until it begins to cook. • Add the chopped garlic, the puréed leaves and the retained cooking water. • Mix well together, bring to the boil, and whisk in the raw egg. • Cook for a couple more minutes and serve.

WILD CHERRY SOUP

1 pint stoned wild cherries
Butter and oil
1½ pints water
Wine
Coriander - ground
Salt and peppercorns
Bread
Sugar [optional]

• Cook ripe cherries very gently in melted butter together with a good pinch of the coriander until they have softened. • Add 1½ pints of water and a glass of red wine or port, a few black peppercorns and pinch of salt. • If the cherries are particularly bitter [they can sometimes be like that] add sugar to taste. • Turn the heat up till the contents of the pan boil, then simmer for another 20-25 minutes.

• Meanwhile, cube the bread for croutons and fry in oil - the addition of garlic is optional. • Sprinkle the croutons over the soup once it is served. If you want the soup thicker add a pinch of flour during the cooking.

JERUSALEM ARTICHOKE & FISH SOUP

Jerusalem artichoke roots
Fish stock [vegetable if unavailable]
Freshwater fish
Spring onion
Salt and pepper
Cream [optional]

• Scrub the artichoke roots and boil in acidulated for about 30 minutes, or until tender. • Discard the cooking water. • Mash the roots and place in a pan with the stock, sliced spring onion and seasoning. • Bring to the boil and then reduce the heat to a rapid simmer. • Add the fish cut into pieces. • Simmer for about 10-15 minutes, or until the fish begins to flake easily. • Serve, stirring in a spot of cream if you have some available.

GLOOPY MALLOW & VEGETABLE OYSTER SOUP

2-3 vegetable oyster / salsify roots [Tragopogon porrifolius]
Butter or oil
2-3 pints common mallow* leaves
1-1½ pints of water
Salt and pepper

In case there is any confusion it should be pointed out that the roots used here are not those of the oysterplant [*Mertensia maritima*] but the vegetable oyster which has the vaguest hint of a fishy taste. Or simply add some flaked fish.

• Begin by slicing the salsify root and plunging into boiling water for 5 minutes, then sweat in a pan with some melted butter. • Chop the mallow leaves and boil with the water for about 10 minutes to release the gloopy content of the leaves. • Add the sweated salsify, cover the pan and simmer for another 10 to 15 minutes.

VARIATIONS
You might also like to try adding some of the naturally occurring herbs which go well with fish - fennel, dill, oregano or marjoram. Garlic will also help.

CHINESE-STYLE VEGETABLE SOUP

Mushrooms
2 tbsp. sesame oil
2 pints spinach-like or wild spring greens
1 ½ pints water [or stock]
Salt and pepper

• Slice and fry a handful of mushrooms gently for about 5 minutes, then remove from the oil. • Cut your chosen spring greens into small pieces and fry for 5 minutes in the oil. • Pour in the water or stock and simmer very gently for 15 to 20 minutes. • Season with salt and pepper.

SWEET CHESTNUT SOUP

Sweet chestnuts
Chicken stock
Butter or oil
Onion [not essential]
Cinnamon, mace and nutmeg
Salt and Pepper
Cream

Sorry, but this is a recipe for those with a caravan or narrowboat kitchen with a blender to hand – unless you have a 'personal blender' to hand... an assistant.

• To make the peeling of the chestnuts easier, make a cut in the skins and then drop into boiling water for a few minutes. • Remove, allow to cool to a manageable temperature, and skin.

• Slice an onion thinly lengthwise and fry in a little butter or oil along with a piece of cinnamon stick, and pinches of mace and nutmeg. • Cook until the onion is softened. • Remove the cinnamon, and add the peeled chestnuts and chicken stock. • Raise the heat to a rolling simmer and cook till the chestnuts are tender. • Remove from the heat, allow to cool, then place in a blender. • Put the purée back in the pan on a low heat, add seasoning to taste, and stir in some cream. Serve.

VARIATIONS
Try adding diced bacon or ham to a spiceless version of this soup.

NETTLE SOUP

1 onion
1 large potato
Butter or oil
1 pint young nettles leaves
1½ pints water
Salt and pepper
Nutmeg
Cream [optional]

• Peel and dice the potato and slice the onion. • Add these to some heated oil in a pan and sweat till they soften. • Chop most of the nettle leaves finely and add to the pan and continue to cook for another 5-10 minutes, stirring the mixture to ensure the nettles are well cooked - but not burnt.

• Pour in the water, bring to the boil and cook until the vegetables are done. In an ideal world – in the comfort of your home - you would probably want to purée the liquid in a blender. • Add the seasoning, spice and a dollop of cream.

VARIATIONS
You might prefer to replace the water with chicken stock. And you may like to hold back a few of the young nettle leaves to be sweated and dropped whole into the final soup.

SWEET CICELY & CHICKEN SOUP

2 onions
Butter or oil
Garlic clove [optional]
Sweet cicely roots
1½ pints chicken stock
Salt and pepper

• Slice the onions, and peel and slice the sweet cicely roots. If you want a slightly more aniseed flavour add a few sweet cicely leaves too.

• Add the onion and garlic to some oil or butter in a pan and sweat till they soften, then add the sweet cicely roots. • Continue to cook the mixture gently for another 10 to 15 minutes, stirring to ensure the vegetables soften evenly, adding a splash of water if the mixture begins to dry too much. • Add seasoning and the chicken stock and simmer for another 15 to 20 minutes. • Depending on whether you like your soup chunky or smooth you may want to blend.

WILDERNESS WATERCRESS SOUP

Butter or oil
1 small onion
Potatoes
Salt and pepper
2-3 handfuls watercress*
1 garlic clove [optional]
1½-2 pints chicken stock [or water]
Cream [optional]

• Dice the potato into small pieces. • Make sure the watercress is well washed, the thicker stalks removed, and then chop roughly. • Finely chop the small onion and sweat in a pan with some butter or oil until softened. • Add the diced potato and seasoning then cook over a medium heat for a few minutes, stirring to stop sticking. • Add the watercress and continue cooking for another minute, before adding the chicken stock. • Bring to the boil and then reduce to a simmer. • Cook for as long as it takes the potato to soften and thicken up the soup.

• Depending on whether you are in a proper kitchen and prefer your soups smooth, then blend, otherwise serve with a little cream stirred in.

ALTERNATIVES
An interesting variation you might like to try is adding real lime juice - not something you will find in Britain's outdoors to be sure - in the last stages before the soup is served. In which case you might like to serve the soup cold as a summer dish.

Consider adding some diced fried bacon when serving, and also some pine nuts, shredded hazlenuts or crushed beech masts.

Other peppery and spicy wild plants that could be used as replacements are lady's smock, bittercress and hedge mustard.

POTATO & LOVAGE SOUP

1 onion
2 large potatoes
Butter or oil
Water
Milk
¼-½ cup lovage* - finely chopped
Salt and pepper

This soup can take on two textures depending on your choice of using lovage leaves, or its blanched stems. Be careful with lovage as it is a potent plant. The first time you try this recipe use just ¼ of a cup to check your tolerance to the herb [see note in the Wild Plant Reference section].

• Finely chop the onion, and peel and dice the potatoes before placing into a pan in which there is some heated oil or butter. • Sweat the vegetables gently for 10 minutes. • Add a couple of cups of water and continue simmering until the potatoes are soft. • Take off the heat.

• Mash the mixture with a fork [or allow to cool and use a blender] then place in pan with the finely chopped lovage leaves or blanched stem. • Add the milk until the liquid reaches the consistency you want then turn up the heat and simmer for a few minutes.

MOCK LEMON SOUP

1 pint chicken stock
1 cup rice
1 tbsp. Japanese knotweed shoots
1 egg
Salt and pepper

Got a friend suffering from a sense of humour failure? Then *really* brighten their day by telling them they are eating Japanese knotweed.

• Put the rice in some boiling stock then reduce the heat to cook until done. • Meanwhile, beat the eggs, and chop the young knotweed stems. • When the rice is almost cooked add the chopped knotweed to the pan and continue cooking for a couple of minutes. • Pour some of the cooking liquor into the beaten egg and whisk, then add this back to the rice. • Stir in thoroughly. • Season with salt and pepper and serve.

NOODLES & HAZELNUT SATAY

Dried egg noodles
Chicken stock

Ground hazelnuts
Milk
Coconut cream
Worcestershire sauce
Hot pepper / chilli sauce

To be honest this recipe was the result of wondering what to do with a small mountain of hazelnuts resting on the kitchen shelf, other than make a dessert or sweet. A little lateral thinking and not a little curiosity led the author to the idea of a hazelnut – as opposed to peanut – satay sauce. The end result was pleasantly surprising and you, too, might be curious enough to try.

• Grind 2 tablespoons of hazelnuts quite finely, but leave granular for texture – just like peanut satay sauce. • Place in a pan with about ½ cup of milk and heat till the milk begins to boil, while stirring. • Turn down the heat and grate, and stir in, about 2 tablespoons of dried coconut cream. • Add a slug of Worcestershire sauce and a few drops of chilli sauce. • Stir and continue cooking for a couple of minutes before reducing the heat right down.

• Meanwhile, place some dried egg noodles in a pan of boiling chicken or other stock. • Boil for a minute, then reduce the heat to a simmer. • Simply allow the noodles to absorb the stock flavour. • Strain off the noodles, place in a dish and spoon over your hazel satay sauce.

BASIC HOMEMADE NOODLES & PASTA

2 tbsp. milk
Flour
1 egg

The aim throughout this guide has been to keep complications and the need for rolled pastry, or pastry of any sort for that matter, to a minimum. However, in the interest of readers who simply cannot survive without noodles in their life, this basic noodle recipe has been added. It does require a means of rolling out the dough and a flat surface to perform the operation, and so won't be a practical proposition to many outdoors people. It also presumes there is an absence of pastry cutters for making fancy shapes.

For basic noodles... • Beat the egg with the milk, and add a pinch of salt. • Add the flour a bit at a time until a stiff dough is formed. • Flour a flat surface and knead the dough before rolling it out very thinly and cutting.

• Depending on what you are preparing drop the pieces into boiling water, stock or bubbling stew. • Cover the pan and continue cooking for 15-20 minutes.

For pasta.... • For a more authentic pasta dough use a ratio of slightly less than 1 cup of a strong plain flour to 1 egg, just over 1 teaspoon of vegetable oil, and a pinch of salt. • Mix and cook in the same way above, although a lot of cooks like their pasta dough to 'rest' for an hour or so before use.

VARIATIONS

What can you do with your pasta? Well you could cut it into narrow spaghetti-like strips, little squares which can be used like ravioli envelopes, wider tagliatelli type forms, or even sheets for a wild food lasagne. You might even consider flavouring the dough.

Creamy and tomato sauces are generally associated with pasta, but how about a pesto made from your favourite wild greens. For a homemade ravioli filling try some minced fish or crushed hazelnuts and bacon, or something like chopped nettles with a bit of cheese. [When forming the final ravioli lightly moisten the edges of one side of the envelope with water or egg and then press together, then allow to dry for about half an hour.]

Sheets of pasta that you prepare for lasagne could also be turned into canelloni, where the pasta is rolled round a stuffing mixture - perhaps a minced rabbit filling with tomato.

In some quick off-the-wall experimentation - in the search for a wild food ravioli dough - the author variously mixed chestnut and acorn flours with both plain and strong wholemeal flour using the pasta dough proportions mentioned above. The results were rather mixed... the dough couldn't be rolled thin enough [perhaps because the impromptu rolling pin was a vinegar bottle!] when using wholemeal flour and the texture was stodgy and heavy when cooked. By far and away better were mixtures of ordinary 'plain' flour with chestnut or acorn. A mix of up to 75% acorn flour to 25% plain flour [3:1] helps the woody, nutty taste of the acorns come through while not becoming heavy and stodgy.

One variation which did work successfully was a chestnut pasta which is used in the CHESTNUT TAGLIATELLI & MUSHROOM recipe, while an acorn and plain flour tagliatelli with a simple mushroom and tomato sauce tasted excellent.

FOR YOUR NOTES

NUTTY & PUDDINGY THINGS

HAZELNUT PUDDING

1 cup hazelnuts - finely chopped / crushed
Pinch of mixed spices [nutmeg, cinnamon]
1 cup caster sugar
3 eggs
Butter

• Mix the spice and crushed or finely chopped nuts [experiment with pine nuts or beech masts too]. • Separate the egg yolks and whites, then mix the yolks with the sugar and combine this with the nut mixture. Mix well. • Take the egg whites, whisk, add to the nut mixture and fold in to add lightness.

• Put mixture into buttered moulds but don't fill right to the top. • Cover with foil or greaseproof paper and place in a steamer or pan of water to steam until cooked - about an hour. You may need to add more water if the pan runs low. • When cooked turn out of the mould and allow to cool.

VARIATIONS
Consider serving with some cream or perhaps a dash of a liquer. And rather than steaming, you could also try baking the pudding altering the cooking time - in a moderate preheated oven probably for about 30-40 minutes. Beech masts can substitute for the hazels.

ACORN & HAZELNUT MACAROONS

¼ cup hazelnuts – ground / finely chopped
¼ cup ground acorn meal or flour
½ cup caster sugar
1-2 egg whites
Cinnamon [optional]

If any of your friends wonder about 'wilderness cooking' then the end product of this recipe should make them stand up and take note! In true macaroons one of the key ingredients is ground almonds. In this recipe these are replaced by a mixture of hazels and acorn meal. The exact proportions of hazelnut and acorn is really up to you, but this a suggested starting point for an unusual variation on the traditional macaroon. The hazels need to be as fine as you can grind them, but allowing for a few larger pieces to add texture to your final macaroons. Edge on the side of more nuts than acorn meal.

• Mix the ground hazelnuts and acorn meal. • Whisk a couple of egg whites until stiff and then whisk in the sugar a small amount at a time. • Fold in

hazel/acorn ingredients a bit at a time – and the cinnamon if you so choose.
• Then place dollops of the mixture on a lightly oiled or greased piece of tin foil
on a baking tray. • Place in a preheated cool oven and cook for 40 to 60
minutes [you really need to keep an eye on this one].

ACORN BISCOTTI

½ cup acorn* mash or meal
¼ cup caster sugar
Baking powder - pinch
1 medium egg
Beech masts or hazelnuts [optional]

Inspired by those Italian biscuits with bits of candied fruit and chopped
almonds, this fatless recipe will let you produce a small batch of acorn-based
cookies. Simply increase the proportions for more. The sugar content here has
been beefed up but it can be reduced.

If using freshly cooked acorn mash squeeze out as much water as possible
before using in this recipe – as the 'flour' component needs to be as dry as
possible. [Dried, ground acorn meal or flour is preferred - a coarse, granulated
sugar-size meal adding a gritty nuttiness to the final result, while a finer flour
will make a smoother end product.]

• In a bowl mix the acorn meal, caster sugar, pinch of baking powder and the
egg. • Adding some nuts for texture is not essential but highly recommended.
• Mix thoroughly together.

• Place dollops of the mixture on a lightly oiled or greased baking tray and
place in an oven just preheated to a cool-moderate setting and bake for 20 to
25 minutes. Higher temperatures will tend to burn the edges of the cookies.

ACORN SPONGE

2 cups mashed acorns*
1 tsp. baking powder
2 egg yolks
½ lb butter
1 cup granulated sugar
1 tsp. each of lemon, almond and vanilla extracts

This is not a sponge in the truest sense, but is thin and has a sponge-like texture.
Normally when making sponge of any kind you are dealing .with dry flour
among the ingredients. And although in the old days acorns were dried and
ground into flour this is rather a laborious exercise when working with a small

batch. So we are working here with a mashed acorn base which is already moist and can potentially make the ingredient mixture rather soft. [*See the Wild Plant Reference section for details on how to prepare acorns.*]

• Squeeze as much water out of the cooked acorns as possible then mash in a bowl. • In a separate bowl cream the butter and sugar. • Separately, mix the eggs and essences then quickly mix in the baking powder. • Mix this thoroughly together and blend into the creamed butter and sugar. • Gradually add the acorn mash and mix until the mixture is well blended.

• Spread the mixture on a baking tray and level off. • Bake for 20-30 minutes in a slow oven, but keeping a keen eye on progress.

SPICY TRAIL MIX

Acorns*
Hazelnuts / beech masts
Dried elderberries
1 tbsp. ground coriander, turmeric
½ tbsp. ground cumin
Salt - good pinch
Cayenne and mustard powder - pinches
Oil

The idea for this trail food comes from that tasty Indian snack Bombay Mix, with the addition of some dried elderberries [collected during the summer months] to provide little bites of sweetness.

• The acorns [as whole as possible] should have been leached and then cool roasted till dry and brittle. • Hazelnuts can be whole or halved. In all you probably want 1-2 pints equivalent of nuts and berries. • Mix all the seasoning ingredients together.

• In a frying pan put the tiniest amount of oil and heat to spread around the bottom of the pan. • Put the main trail food ingredients in the pan and gently heat, stirring to distribute a little of the oil on the nuts and berries. • Sprinkle the seasoning over and continue to warm. The idea is not to fry the ingredients but to coat them and infuse some of the flavours. • Allow to cool then store in a cool place.

ALTERNATIVES

Another item you might like to add to trail food mix is sweet chestnut. Slice uncooked nuts across their width - you will lose the top and bottom, but should get about three segments. Allow these to partly dry out for a few hours then lightly fry in a little oil to crispen up. [The author used this method to cook some sweet chestnuts that were still green but emerging from their prickly husks.] Discard the outer skin, which will easily separate after frying, and then add the pieces to the rest of your trail mix. Also consider adding some ACORN SEV to your trail mix.

CANDIED NUTS & ACORNS

Acorns*
Beech masts
Pine nuts
Hazelnuts
Sugar

This is a quick recipe for transforming nutty items from the hedgerow into candies. • In the case of acorns they must first have been leached, boiled then dried, or cool roasted until brittle.

• Simply place some sugar in a pan and melt until it begins to turn a very light golden colour - one or two drops of water can help start the melting process. • Stir continuously so the sugar is not fully caramelized - unless that is a taste you prefer. • Stir the nuts into the sugar and make sure they are coated properly. • Remove individually with a fork and place on a plate or mesh rack to cool and harden. With beech masts it can be a bit fiddly to separate them individually so leave them in small clumps.

STEWED DAMSONS

Bullaces or damsons
Water
Sugar
Cornflour [optional]

The very tart tasting damson - a domesticated version of the bullace, but now largely forgotten - will provide you with lots of vitamins C and E and can often be found growing wild in our hedgerows.

• To exploit this natural wild resource simply place the damsons in a pan with water, in a rough ratio of 1 pint to 1 lb. of fruit. • Bring to the boil and then gently simmer until tender. • The sugar can be dissolved in the boiling water or added when serving. • If you prefer the juice a bit thicker then mix a few teaspoonfuls of cornflour with water and add during the boiling stage, maintaining the heat until the cornflour has cooked through and begun to thicken the juices.

HAZELNUT CRUNCH

1/2 cup sugar
1/2 cup hazelnuts - chopped

This one of the simplest ways of providing something sugary to nibble when en-route outdoors. That said, there are different outcomes depending on your personal taste.

In both cases the sugar needs to be melted in a pan - just enough heat applied to melt the sugar but not caramelize, unless that is your preference. A few drops of water can help start the melting process.

Simply stir the hazels into the sugar.... for brittle sugary chunks roughly chop or crunch the nuts, combine with the molten sugar and then pour onto a piece of kitchen foil. Allow to mixture to cool then break into chunks.

The second alternative is to grind the hazels quite finely, before adding to the sugar and stirring in. The molten sugar is very quickly absorbed by the hazel grounds and takes on a crumble-like consistency. Again, turn out onto kitchen foil to cool. This method doesn't produce large clumps but smaller crumble-like beads of crunchy sugared hazel. Sprinkle over salads or sweets for an exotic taste of the wild.

VARIATIONS
Try adding a little cinnamon or nutmeg to the mixture.

MINTED PEARS

Ripe pears
White wine
Honey
Vinegar

'Friends, Romans, countryfolk. Lend me your pears...'

If you are fortunate enough to come across some wild pears in the wilderness here is a method of preparing them - particularly since wild pears are often a bit gritty and not always very sweet. Incidentally, the inspiration for this recipe comes from an old Roman text.

• Peel, quarter and core the pears. • Place in a pan with pan with a sprig of mint, good dollop of honey, small splash of vinegar, and enough white wine to almost cover the fruit. • Bring to the boil, cover, reduce heat and simmer for about 20 minutes, or until the pears are tender. • Allow to cool then serve. • If the sauce is a little too liquid remove the pears and reduce the sauce.

VARIATIONS
Red wine may also be used, and in this case rather than using the mint substitute a piece of cinnamon stick and some cloves, and serve with a little pepper.

DAMSON & BLACKBERRY CRUMBLE

Damsons
Blackberries
Sugar
2 cups plain flour
2½ heaped tbsp. brown sugar
3 heaped tbsp. butter
1 tsp. baking powder
Spices [optional]

Crumbles can be a very simple [even simpler if you buy a ready-made crumble mixture] way of producing a dessert, and in this case to exploit two of our best-known wild fruits, damsons and blackberries.

• Make the crumble by adding the baking powder to the flour in a mixing bowl then adding the butter. • Rub the butter into the flour to produce breadcrumb-like beads of fatted flour. • Once the butter has been evenly distributed add the sugar and stir in. The sugar can be soft brown or demerara type, but even caster would do.

• Spread the damsons and blackberries evenly in the bottom of a pie dish. • Add a couple of tablespoons of sugar and any spice [cinnamon, for example] then cover evenly with the crumble mixture, patting it gently down. • Bake for 30 to 40 minutes in a pre-heated moderate to moderately-hot oven.

SPICY KNOTWEED CRUMBLE

Cooking or crab-apples
Japanese knotweed stems
Cinnamon, ginger and nutmeg - pinches
Ground clove - pinch
Apple or orange juice

This recipe takes advantage of the lemony flavour of knotweed. For the crumble topping see the previous recipe above. Use a ratio of about 4:1 apples to knotweed stems. Crab-apples will need sugar adding to reduce tartness.

• Trim the knotweed stems and, if necessary, peel. • Core and slice the apples.
• Place both ingredients in a baking dish and sprinkle pinches of the spices

over. • Drizzle a little apple or orange juice over then cover with crumble mixture. • Bake for 30-40 minutes in a pre-heated moderate to moderately-hot oven.

SWEET BARLEY BAKE

1 cup barley
1 pint water
Fruit of choice
Sugar [optional]

This is a very simple way of making a sweet out of any untamed, but ripened, barley which you find in the wild. At a push this could recipe could also be cooked in double thickness foil with a campfire.

• Remove any apparently diseased grains then roughly rub off as much of the husk as possible and wash. • Put the grains in a small baking dish and pour the water over them. • Place in a preheated slow oven and cook for about 2 hours. • Depending on the type of fruit you want to add slice or chop and fold into the baking barley 20-30 minutes before cooking completion.

The addition of sugar is optional and may be determined on the type and sweetness of the fruit available locally.

BILBERRY FRITTERS

Bilberries
Flour
Salt
Spices [optional]
Fruit Juice - or milk or water
Butter
Caster Sugar

The hills are alive with the sound of... f-r-y-i-n-g.

If you are in the uplands from July through September and you come across bilberries, what better time to pick a few and do something inspiring with them? Bilberry pudding and pies are traditional ways of cooking the fruit, but this recipe will let you enjoy the fruit in simple fritter form.

• Place some flour with a pinch of salt in a bowl and mix. If you want to include any spices that go well with fruit then this is the time. • Add some milk or water, and a splash of natural fruit juice if you have some, and stir to create a quite thick but smooth batter mixture. • Add your bilberries.

• In a frying pan place a good chunk of butter and heat till very hot. • Spoon in dollops of the bilberry batter mixture and fry, making sure that both sides get the heat treatment. • Remove, drain off any remaining butter and sprinkle with sugar.

ALTERNATIVES
Another fritter option you might like to try are sliced or chopped hazelnuts in batter, and spiced or sugared according to preference. This is one way of dealing with unripened hazels.

ELDER FLOWER FRITTERS

Elder flowers
2 cups of flour
2 eggs
1 tbsp. milk
Pinch of salt
Oil
Sugar

Yet another type of wild food fritter, but this time using the fragrant flowery heads of the elder.

• Mix the flour, eggs, milk and salt in a bowl to produce a batter. • Dunk bunches of flowers into the batter [make sure the flowers are dry first] then drop into hot oil and fry until lightly golden brown [pan frying in butter is not really satisfactory for these fritters since you need to quickly seal and cook the florets]. • Remove florets from the hot oil, allow to drain, and sprinkle with sugar.

SWEET CHESTNUT FRITTERS

Sweet chestnuts - mashed
Salt
Hazelnuts
Dried fruit
Butter

This is a batterless recipe. • Bake or boil some chestnuts and then mash into an almost dry paste. • Add chopped hazelnuts and/or dried fruit of choice and a pinch of salt. • Mix everything together thoroughly. • Form into flattened cakes and pan fry in butter until brown. • Dust with caster sugar and serve with a little drizzle of fruit juice.

CHESTNUT PANCAKE LAYER-CAKE

Chestnut meal
Eggs
Milk
Baking powder
Salt - pinch
Marmalade or honey

This recipe began with some excursions into replacing ordinary flour in a pancake recipe with some finely mashed chestnut meal. Although equal proportions of chestnut, egg and milk will produce a pancake, they are rather delicate but do have naturally sweetish edge to them. Reducing the milk content a little will produce a sturdier end product.

• Mix chestnut meal, eggs and milk. • For every cup of batter add a pinch of baking powder and salt, then mix this thoroughly in. • Heat some oil in a pan and pour in small amounts of the batter. • Allow the first side to cook until golden brown before flipping over to do the other side. • Prepare several more similar sized pancakes.

• Next, lightly oil or grease a round oven dish similar in size to your pancakes [or simply produce the pancakes to size.] • Place one pancake flat in the bottom of the dish and then smear some marmalade or honey on [soft fruits could be used too]. • Repeat the process of layering the pancakes. • Place in a moderate oven and bake for another 15-20 minutes. • Remove from the oven and allow to cool for ten minutes, then slice and serve.

CHESTNUT & APPLE PUD

Sweet chestnuts
Cooking apples
Sugar

Ahhh... another touch of comfort food. Especially with cream! Ice cream! A sprinkling of dates perhaps... or a splash of liquer. Dream on!

• Peel, core and stew some apples until they are very soft. • Meanwhile, skin the chestnuts, halve or slice, and gently boil till tender. • When cooked add to the stewed apple and stir in. • Allow to rest for 5 minutes then serve.

FIRE BAKED CRAB-APPLES

Crab-apples
Sugar [preferably brown]
Dried fruits
Allspice
Butter

Although this has a couple of untypical ingredients the recipe offers a simple method for cooking with the most basic campfire.

• Halve the crab-apples, remove the core and then sandwich the apple halves together again. • Place on some tin foil which will be used to form an envelope round the apples [fold the foil double to provide more strength]. • Sprinkle the apples with plenty of brown sugar, a pinch of allspice [or the equivalent of mixed ground cloves, cinnamon and nutmeg], some dried fruits such as elderberries or currants, and a couple of knobs of butter.

• Seal up the foil envelope and then place over embers or where the apples can be cooked nice and slowly, or even bury the foil envelope in ashes. • Bake for about 10 minutes, then check and bake longer if required.

CRAB-APPLE or BLACKBERRY PANCAKES

Crab-apples / blackberries
Sugar
1 ¼ cups flour
2 cups milk
2 eggs
Butter and Oil

• Halve the crab-apples, remove the core material and then slice finely. • Place a small knob of butter in a pan, melt, then put in the apple pieces and a little sugar. • Heat to soften the apples and warm them a little. • Take off the heat.

• Put all the flour, milk and egg ingredients in a bowl and stir until a smooth batter forms. • Put a little oil in a frying or pancake pan and heat until the oil is very hot and evenly coating the pan. • Put about a third of a cup of the batter mixture in the pan and tip so that it swishes round evenly. • About a minute on each side should cook. Serve with the apples or blackberries wrapped in the pancake.

VARIATION
If you have dried any red clover flowers, try crushing them into a meal and adding to the batter as part of the flour component. The apples could also be grated and then cooked.

CHESTNUT MERINGUES

Chestnut meal
Egg whites
Sugar [caster preferred]

These 'meringues' are nothing like the ones you will normally associate with but are an interesting way of making use of those leftover egg whites. In terms of proportions you will want about a heaped dessert spoon of chestnut meal [this gives a nice nutty texture] to each egg white.

• Beat the egg whites until stiff. • Sprinkle over the chestnut meal and fold in gently. • The lay spoonfuls of the mixture on a lightly greased piece of foil on a baking tray. • Dust with caster sugar and cook in a preheated slow oven for about an hour.

VARIATIONS
If you want a really sweet meringue that is more traditional then sugar needs to be beaten in with the egg whites at the start. There is obviously scope for more savoury variations to accompany main courses. For something more exotic consider placing a small piece of chocolate inside each meringue before baking.

CANDIED VIOLETS

Violet flowers
Egg white
Caster sugar

Something for the home cook, but making use of the excellent vitamin content in violet flowers and which you can use to garnish a wild food pud.

• Collect flowers and remove stalk material. • Gently rise in cold water then softly dry with tissue paper. • Beat the egg white to aerate but not to a meringue consistency. • Dip the flowers in the egg and then sprinkle liberally with sugar. • Put on foil or greaseproof paper and allow to dry in a cool place for a couple of days. • Store in a sealed jar [they should keep for 3-4 weeks].

ALTERNATIVES
The same process can be applied to the flowers of primrose.

FOR YOUR NOTES

SAUCEY THINGS

BILBERRY CHUTNEY

1 onion
Ground ginger, cinnamon, cayenne and salt
½ cup vinegar [flavoured preferred]
½ cup sugar
3-4 cups bilberries

Out on the hills? Then consider gathering some bilberries for making a chutney for future use with game meats.

• Chop the onion and place in a pan with pinches of ground ginger and cinnamon, cayenne pepper and salt, plus the vinegar. • Ordinary vinegar is fine but a cider or raspberry vinegar will add more flavour. • Bring these ingredients to the boil, then simmer for about 15 minutes before adding almost all the bilberries [keep a handful or two back for adding final texture].

• Continue stirring and simmering for about 20 minutes, then add the fruit which you kept back, and simmer for 10 minutes. • Take off the heat, allow to cool and then bottle - either in sterile jars for long term storage or non-sterile jars for keeping in the refrigerator short-term.

BILBERRY SAUCE

2 cups bilberries
Water
Sugar
Lemon juice [optional]
Cornflour

A simple and quick wild fruit sauce which can be served alongside pheasant, pigeon or other game meats.

• Put the bilberries, together with a handful of sugar, slug of water and, optionally, a splash of lemon juice, into a pan and bring to the boil. • Reduce the heat and simmer for about 10 minutes.

• Dissolve a couple of teaspoons of cornflour in some water and add to the simmering ingredients. • Stir in and continue cooking until the sauce thickens.

DAMSON & ONION SAUCE

Damsons
Fresh orange juice
Sugar
Onions

• Quickly cut the damson flesh to the stones to speed up the cooking time.
• Combine with orange juice and a handful of sugar in a pan and cook till
tender. • Meanwhile, slice the onion very thinly and gently fry till softened and
browned. • Add the cooked damsons and stir in and then strain or sieve the
whole mass, pushing some of the pulp through the sieve to thicken the sauce.
Good with game meat like pheasant.

WILD CHERRY SAUCE

2 cups wild cherries
Water
½ pint stock [chicken or vegetable]
Handful of dried elder or juniper* berries
Sugar
Salt
Butter
1 tbsp. flour

This sauce is an accompaniment for game dishes. • Remove stones then simmer
the cherries gently in a little water till they soften. • Strain the juice in a sieve
then force the cherries through the mesh and recombine with the juice.
• Add the stock, a pinch of sugar and salt.

• Blend a large knob of butter with a tablespoon of flour, then add a few
spoonfuls of the cherry liquid to dilute. • Place this mixture back with the sauce.
• Stir everything thoroughly together, bring the contents of the pan to the boil
and then simmer - reducing until the desired consistency is achieved.

SORREL SAUCE

Sorrel* leaves - de-stalked
Butter
Flour
Single cream
Salt and pepper

The sorrel leaf can be an effective tangy replacement for lemon. • In a pan wilt
some leaves in melted butter and reduce. • Add a good pinch of ordinary flour

and stir this in and cook for a few minutes more. • Add your cream a bit at a time while still stirring [but don't overheat which will cause the cream to curdle]. • Cook until the sauce thickens up then add seasoning to taste. Good with trout and salmon.

HORSERADISH & CRAB-APPLE SAUCE

½-1 cup grated horseradish* root
1 lb crab apples
1 tbsp. sugar
1 cup vinegar

Both tart and hot this makes a good accompaniment for the potentially lack-lustre bream.

• Grate the horseradish and peeled crab-apples [cooking apples will also do], and add the sugar. • Stir in half of the vinegar and begin to work in, adding the remainder a bit at a time until a creamy consistency is achieved. • Refrigerate.

COCONUT & MINT SAUCE

Coconut cream
Mint – chopped
1 garlic clove
Green chilli [optional]
Sugar or clear honey
Lemon juice
Oil

This little sauce or dip mixture can either be spicy hot to accompany a meat dish, or left sweet and minty as a salad dressing.

• Crumble some coconut cream into a little boiling water and dissolve.
• Meanwhile crush the garlic, preferably pasting it. • Very finely chop the mint.
• If opting for the chilli de-seed and chop very finely. • Place mint in a bowl with a little sugar, and the garlic then crush everything together with the back of a spoon. • Add lemon juice and some oil, and then the coconut. • Mix well.

VARIATIONS
If you're really stuck for mint and sugar in the field consider crumbling and melting some Kendal mint cake.... 'Awww,' you say, 'That's no way to treat KMC!' Oh well, only a thought.

ROSE HIP JELLY

Rose hips
Water
Sugar

• Gather the best hips you can find, remove the beards and stems, and split them in half lengthwise, and place into a pan with water - approx. 1:1 ratio of water to hips. • Cover and cook till tender, adding more water as required. • When done, remove from the heat and strain through fine muslin, but don't squeeze any of the pulp through as this will make your jelly cloudy. • Measure the resulting liquid and add 1 lb of sugar for every pint of liquid. • Place back on the heat and boil until the jelling point is reached [see ELDERBERRY JELLY recipe below].

ELDERBERRY JELLY

1 lb stripped elderberries
1 lb crab-apples [or cookers]
¾ pint water
1 lb sugar
Cinnamon stick

This lovely jelly can be used as a jam or to accompany game dishes.

• Halve the crab-apples lengthways and place with the elderberries [which are easily stripped from their stalks using a fork] in a pan with the water. • Bring to the boil, cover, then simmer for around 20 to 30 minutes when the mass should have become pulpy. If you are using cooking apples you will need to quarter them to quicken cooking.

• Place the pulp in a fine sieve or piece of muslin and let the juice drip through until it stops dripping. Don't force through any of the pulp as this will cloud the jelly. • Place the juice in a pan and stir in and dissolve the sugar - working to a rough proportion of 1 pint of simmered juice to 1 lb of sugar. • Bring to the boil then turn down the heat to continue at a good simmer until 'set' - generally within 15 to 30 minutes. [The setting point can be tested for after 15 minutes by putting a little of the juice on a cold plate. After a few minutes the juice should have jelled.] • Pour into hot jars sterilized in an oven.

VARIATIONS
The berries of the rowan, or mountain ash, can similarly be made into a jelly. Use a ratio of 2 lb rowan, 1 lb apples, 1 pint of water and 1 ½ lb of sugar.

CRAB-APPLE JELLY

1½ lb crab apples
1½ cups water
2 cups sugar

This recipe will produce about 1 pint of jelly. • Select good quality apples, three quarters of which should be fully ripe, the others firm. • Simply de-stem the apples, cut into pieces and place with the water in a pan. • Cover, bring to the boil then reduce heat and simmer for about 25 minutes or when the apples are soft.

• Put the pulp in a sieve or piece of muslin to extract the juice. If you don't want a cloudy jelly let the pulp drain naturally without forcing through the mesh. You should get about 2 cups of juice.

• Place the juice in pan and add the sugar. • Boil at a high heat. • When the mixture gels on a cold plate it is ready. • Remove from the heat and pour into hot sterilized jars. Leave a little space at the top and cap.

ELDERBERRY SYRUP

1 lb elderberries
2 pints boiling water
1 lb caster sugar

• Strip ripe elderberries from their stalks with a fork. • Place in a pan and crush with the back of a spoon. • Add the boiling water and leave overnight. • Strain into another pan through muslin or a fine sieve then stir in the sugar. • Bring to the boil then reduce heat to a gentle boil and heat until the liquid becomes syrupy. • Allow to cool, then bottle and keep the bottles chilled in the fridge.

ROSE HIP PURÉE

Rose hips - seeded
Water

This purée can be added to soups and stews or used as an accompaniment to salmon or meat.

• Remove the tops and tails of the rose hips, and their seeds. • Place in a pan and add 1 cup of water for each cup of prepared rose hips. • Bring to the boil, cover, and then reduce to a simmer, adding a little more water if required. • Cook until the hips can be mashed - or use a blender.

ROSE HIP SYRUP

1 pint rose hips
1 pint water
2 cups sugar

• Select some nice, blemish-free rose hips. • Nip off the beards and any stalk material, and slit down the centre. • Put the water and sugar in a pan and boil until the sugar dissolves. • Add the rose hips and simmer gently for about an hour, topping up with boiling water if it gets too low in the pan.

• Take off the heat and place in a metal sieve. • Express the juicy syrup by pressing with the back of a spoon but don't force any pulp through the sieve mesh - that will cloud your syrup. • Allow to cool, bottle and keep in a fridge for longer-term storage.

MINT SYRUP

1 handful mint leaves
2 cups sugar
1 cup water
½ cup vinegar
½ cup lemon juice

The Iranians make a mint syrup as the basis of a cool drink which you may find refreshing during the hot summer – assuming there happens to be one.

• Boil the sugar and water to dissolve the sugar, turn down the heat and add the vinegar and lemon juice and boil at a reduced heat for about 15 minutes - or until the liquid is becomes syrupy. • Remove from the heat, add the mint leaves and allow to cool. • Bottle, and store in a fridge for longer term keeping.

RASPBERRY VINAIGRETTE

Raspberries [or blackberries]
1 part vinegar
4 parts olive oil
1 garlic clove
French mustard [optional]

This variation sweetens the traditional French dressing and can be used with wild leaf salads.

• Express the juice of the raspberries or blackberries in a cup or bowl and strain off the liquid, avoiding any pips. • Add to the other ingredients as they are mixed for the dressing.

HORSERADISH SAUCE - PICKLED / CREAMED

Horseradish* - grated
Salt
Sugar
Pinch pickling spices [optional]
Vinegar - preferably spirit

First the pickling method.... • Place the vinegar, sugar and salt in a pan, stir and bring to the boil. • Take off the heat and stir in the grated horseradish. • Bottle.

If the horseradish is particularly strong and pungent you may like to consider adding the grated root just before removing the pan from the heat. However, the aim is not to cook the root but just drive off some of the pungency and oils through quickly heating the grated root. Now to version two...

Horseradish* - grated
Cream
Lemon juice
Sugar [optional]
Salt
Oil

This is a more traditional creamed horseradish sauce. • Use a thick cream and stir the grated root into it, adding a splash of lemon juice and salt. • If the root is very pungent you might like to add a teaspoon of sugar. • Combine thoroughly then dribble in olive oil, beating it into the mixture to produce a smooth emulsion. • Make just enough for your immediate needs.

BROOM PICKLES OR CAPERS

Broom* flower buds
Wine vinegar
Bay leaves
Cloves
Peppercorns
Salt

You will have noticed in the *Wild Plant Reference section* a mention of broom pickles. This is one method to prepare them.

• Place the vinegar, bay leaves, several cloves, a few peppercorns and salt in a pan, bring to the boil then turn down to a low simmer. • Add tightly closed broom flower buds and continue to simmer for a couple of minutes - but don't overcook. • Remove from the heat, allow to cool and bottle. • You can use these pickles like capers as they did many centuries ago when huge quantities of broom pickles were prepared.

VARIATIONS
Drain some of the pickles and add to mayonnaise. Try serving with baked potatoes and soured cream.

BLACKBERRY KETCHUP

3 pints blackberries
2 cups brown sugar
1 cup vinegar
1 tsp. ground cloves and cinnamon
Pinch of allspice

• Very slowly cook the fruit, spices and vinegar for 2 hours by which time the mass should be soft. • Take off the heat. • You can blend the whole mass or you can force it through a sieve to remove the blackberry pips - on the other hand if you are out in the field you might not care about that. • Bottle.

CRAB-APPLE KETCHUP

2-3 pints crab-apples
1 cup sugar
Salt and pepper
Ground cloves, cinnamon, mustard powder
2 onions
1 pint vinegar

• Halve the crab-apples, and remove the core and stalk material. • Place in a stainless steel pan, add just enough water to cover and simmer very gently for about 30 minutes - or until the apples are soft and water almost gone. • Remove from the heat and rub through a sieve into another pan.

• Add good pinches of salt, pepper, ground cloves, cinnamon and mustard powder, plus finely chopped onions, and the vinegar. • Bring to the boil, cover and then simmer for an hour. • Bottle in sterilized jars or freeze in plastic containers for longer term storage.

WILD MUSTARD SAUCE

Dried wild mustard seed
Flour
Water
Vinegar

• Lightly brown some plain flour on a tray in the oven. • Meanwhile grind the dried seeds of black* or white mustard. • Add the flour and then equal proportions of water and vinegar. • Stir into a smooth paste. All of the component ingredients can be adjusted to suit personal preferences.

VARIATIONS
Try adding a little grated horseradish* to the mixture. You might also like to try experimenting with various wild plant alternatives to the mustard - the peppery seed pods of shepherd's purse, for example, or the seeds of charlock.

TEA-LIKE THINGS

While out and about you may want a hot drink, and the wilderness larder can provide some ingredients for these too - to be used in tisanes or teas. There is a subtle difference between the two. Tisanes are made by infusing hot water with fresh or dried leaves, while teas are made from the partly fermented leaves of plants.

One of the problems with creating drinks from wild plants is that this is verging on the area of herbal medicine, and that is not what this guide is about. What's more, drinking an infusion is very much akin to drinking the water you might have cooked your wild plants in, and that water may contain substances which have contra-indications for some people.

If you are driving, or involved in some essential outdoor activity, the last thing you want to be drinking is something that makes you sleepy. In this particular respect you should not make tisanes from chamomile, hops, red clover flowers or valerian.

A very important point about tisanes and teas is that you use fresh or dried leaves of pre-flowering plants, and NOT pick yellowed or dead leaves. When they turn brown the leaves of many plants develop hydrocyanic acid which is in the same family of chemicals as cyanide, and is what makes the leaves in autumn turn brown. So only use properly dried leaves [*see the introduction to the recipes section*], and avoid yellow, browned or dead leaves.

As for quantities, use 1 teaspoon of dried leaves or 2 to 3 teaspoons of fresh leaves and infuse in ¼-pint of boiling water for anything from a couple of minutes up to ten, then strain off the leaves or flowers.

Borage - use leaves and flowers [mildly diuretic]
Elder flowers - soak in lemon juice overnight for a cold summer drink, or a teaspoon of dried flowers added to ordinary tea
Ground Ivy – bitter leaves once dried and used as a tea
Lime - infusions of the flowers are the so-called 'Linden Tea' [potentially sedative], or 1 to 2 teaspoons of dried flowers added to a mug of boiling water
Meadowsweet - use flowers
Mint
Nettles - leaves [nettles may reduce blood-sugar and blood pressure]
Peppermint - use leaves
Pine needles - requires 10-15 minutes infusion but full of vitamin C
Rosehips

COOKING IN THE WILD

The ordinary camper, unless they are in a caravan with a fully equipped kitchen, is generally limited to cooking by boiling and frying. With a little effort and imagination as well as some knowledge the limits can be expanded quite considerably. An open fire presents a 'different' challenge, but opens up more opportunities - and more fun! - such as baking and roasting which can be done in the ashes of a fire. Food can even be buried 'under' the fire as one of the author's friends describes in this information on hangis and yukon stoves....

There are other methods for improving how we cook over open fires and here we look at two - the Yukon Stove and the Hangi. There are also a number of suggested items that may be useful for the techniques described below:

	Item	Qty	Use / Remarks
1	Digging tool	1	Getting earth and mud
2	Steel plate - 30 x 30cm	1	Hot plate on top
3	Steel mesh - 30 x 30cm	1	Grill
4	Metal biscuit tin	1	Oven, instead of hot plate or 'smoking box'

THE YUKON STOVE

Heat from a camp fire can be channelled by making a 'Yukon Stove' where the fire is surrounded by a wall of turf blocks or mud and stones, with a flat surface over part of the top. The stove is fed from another hole at the base; sometimes recessed in the ground to shield the fire source from the wind. With a bit of experience it is quite quick to build though the mud and stone versions do need time to set and dry before use.

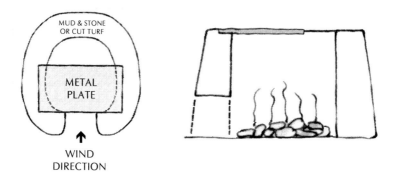

MUD & STONE OR CUT TURF

METAL PLATE

WIND DIRECTION

MODIFIED YUKON STOVE DESIGN

THE HANGI

Pacific Islanders have a technique known as a 'hangi' where food is parcelled up in leaves, placed on hot stones then buried for several hours to steam... It was also applied in less hospitable times past to missionaries curious enough to set foot on those distant shores.

The sizes and dimensions here are suitable for something about the size of a whole sheep!

Remove turf from an area 4 x 3 feet and set aside. Dig to depth of at least 18 inches, keep the spoil for covering the cooking food. Build a fire to cover the floor of the pit, layering smooth rounded stones between layers of fuel wood. Since palms and/or banana trees are a rare commodity outside the tropics, cooking foil is an acceptable substitute for wrapping your food in and, unlike leaves, foil can even be reused with care.

Light the fire, and when it has burnt down, rake the stones to cover the pit floor. Drive a few green branches vertically into the ashes. Load your parcelled food onto the hot stones and bury with the earth. Pull out the branches and pour a small quantity of water into the channels formed by the removed branches to generate steam. Seal the holes, continue partying for a few hours.

A whole sheep will need 5–6 hours to cook. Cooking time is reduced by making smaller parcels, but leave for at least 2 hours to tenderize. Dinner is served whenever you wish to dig for it. After the party, burn off the rubbish and re-cover the hole with the turf put to one side at the start.

THE SMOKING BOX

This is best for hot smoking fish or small game. Layer the base of a biscuit tin with sawdust or leaves from suitable trees. Unless you particularly like the taste of resin, do NOT use pine needles. Oak or beech is best.

Place the food to be smoked on some mesh raised above the smoking material. The meat or fish should be thinly spread and clean, with little or no fat attached.

Cover gently with the lid and place on warm ashes of the fire. The idea is not to set the wood or leaves in the tin alight, but just to let them smoulder away. Leave for a couple of hours. The time required needs experimentation. Squirrels done this way are tasty but very tough! Oily fish like mackerel is good. Meat and fish cooked this way will keep for a few days, especially if well salted before smoking.

OTHER TIPS FOR WOULD-BE WILDERNESS COOKS

• Chicken wire is a useful foldable material which can be used to envelop fish or other awkward foodstuffs during cooking, or provide a lightweight grill for cooking food over a fire. Depending on the weight of the food item to be cooked the mesh may need doubling up, or extra support be provided.

• Wild fish can be simply cooked on a stick held over a fire, but how do you cook a stuffed fish [without the aid of the chicken wire above]? The answer is to select three straight-ish green twigs or small branches that will reach across the width of your fire. Make sure to use green wood and strip the bark. Then place two of the twigs side by side on a flat surface - the distance apart depending on the size of the fish to be cooked. Place the fish on top then lay the third twig on top of this.

The next step is to crimp the free twig ends together so they trap the fish tightly. This could be simply done with string, or from thick grasses or small flexible twigs twisted into loops, then slipped over the twig ends and slid towards the food. Obviously you cannot place the fish into the fire but if you keep the twigs out of the flames they should survive long enough to see your fish cooked, and you can always wet the twigs.

• In real emergencies some items like bread dough can be wrapped round a bark-stripped stick and baked over a fire.

• Recipes within this guide sometimes call for an oven or baking dish. In the absence of the real thing in the outdoors a rudimentary reusable baking dish can be fashioned from kitchen foil. Reinforcement can come from that chicken wire.

Fold a longish piece of foil several times lengthwise to increase the number of layers and strength, then 'form' your dish round the bottom of a pan. The dish will be strong enough to support lighter weight meals that need to be baked in an oven. Keep the dull foil side facing the heat source.

• Another alternative is to line a metal handled pan with a folded double layer of foil; pushing into the curves while avoiding breaking the foil. Place the pan in oven and leave the corners of the foil sticking up to use as handles when removing the finished meal for serving. If the pan is thin sided, then cooking time and temperature may well need to be amended to prevent burning of food around the edges.

• For recipes like meatloaf, burgers or fish cake mixes you can always cook the same ingredients by rolling them in foil like a thick sausage. Make sure that the foil overlaps at least once, then twist the ends closed. Boil, bake or steam the contents as circumstances dictate.

• Another alternative is to line a metal handled pan with a folded double layer of foil; pushing into the curves while avoiding breaking the foil. Place the pan in oven and leave the corners of the foil sticking up to use as handles when removing the finished meal for serving. If the pan is thin sided, then cooking time and temperature may well need to be amended to prevent burning of food around the edges.

• For recipes like meatloaf, burgers or fish cake mixes you can always cook the same ingredients by rolling them in foil like a thick sausage. Make sure that the foil overlaps at least once, then twist the ends to close. Boil, bake or steam the contents as circumstances dictate.

• Stumped for something to 'mash' an ingredient with? Solved by finding a stick from a non-poisonous shrub or tree, removing the bark, squaring off the end and then using as a masher. Granted a bit slower than a proper potato masher.

• Should you decide to treat yourself to a wild lasagne or ravioli in your outdoors kitchen you can always roll the pasta dough using a clean bottle or even one of the larger mini-sized camping gas cylinders. Primitive, to be sure, but expedient.

• Really stuck for something to cook on? Then always consider the hollow of a spade – well cleaned, of course. The author was recently told a story about a builder who carried a separate spade in the back of his van, and swathed in protective cloth. At lunchtime the brightly polished spade would emerge from its hiding place, be thrust over the ubiquitous building slte fire and a bacon and egg fry-up ensue. Now you know!

• Kebab skewers can be fashioned from the dry twigs of non-poisonous trees or shrubs [hazel, sweet chestnut, sycamore, birch or beech for example] which has had the bark removed.

• Simple mixing vessels can be fashioned out of the bottom of PET soft drink bottles. Plastic bags can also be used for mixing ingredients. Be wary when using tin cans as mixing or cooking vessels as the galvanizing may be scraped into your food with a sharp implement, and some metal cans are lined with a thin plastic film.

• Two sheets of plastic film, or a clean old carrier bag, are ideal for making your own tortillas. In the absence of proper masa harina use cooked polenta rolled into balls slightly larger than a golf ball. Place between the plastic sheets and roll out until about the thickness of a pencil lead. Peel off the plastic and dry fry the tortilla blanks on both sides until they are speckled with brown marks.

COOKING TEMPERATURE EQUIVALENTS

The aim of this guide has been to simplify the cooking process so readers without access to sophisticated equipment can feed themselves. For anyone happening to have access to more technology the table below shows equivalent oven temperatures.

Gas Mark	Oven temperature	F° / C°
¼	Very Cool	225° / 110°
½		250° / 120°
1	Cool	275° / 140°
2		300° / 150°
3	Moderate	325° / 160°
4		350° / 180°
5	Moderately hot	375° / 190°
6		400° / 200°
7	Hot	425° / 220°
8		450° / 230°
9	Very hot	475° / 250°

THE ROUGH FRESHWATER FISH GUIDE

A very quick approximation of the flavours and eating characteristics of key freshwater fish that readers may encounter in the wild.

BARBEL	Very bony	Tasteless	Bake, braise, grill or poach with lots of flavouring.
BREAM	Bony with soft flesh	Bland	Braise, stew. Add strong flavours
CARP	Meaty flesh	Delicate	Bake, braise, stuff. Season strongly.
CHAR	Firm pink or white flesh	Delicate	Bake, barbecue, braise, fry, grill or poach.
CHUB	Bony – small	Poor eating	Bake, grill, stock.
DACE	Very bony	Unexciting	Deep fry, stock, mince.
GRAYLING	Firm white flesh	Briefly thyme-scented. Trout-like taste.	Bake, grill, pan-fried or potted.
GUDGEON	Small	Delicate and excellent	Deep fry
PERCH	Firm white flesh	Delicate – prized	Small - pan/deep-fry. Large - bake, grill, poach, stuff.
ROACH	Full of bones. Firm flesh	Unexciting	Bake, grill, pan-fry.
RUDD		Poor	Stock
PIKE	Sharp bones. Soft white flesh sometimes dry. Avoid eating roe.	Delicate	Bake, braise, grill steaks, poach, stuff.
TENCH	Very slimy skin.	Quite good	Bake, braise, grill, stew, stuff. Smaller fish fried.
TROUT	Succulent	Good	Bake, fry, grill.
ZANDER	Meaty, but flaky and soft.	Good	Bake, grill, poach, stuff.

THE QUICK HERB GUIDE

This quick guide shows you which herbs can go well with which meats, ingredients and dishes.

	STOCK	SALADS	SOUPS	SAUCES	EGG DISHES	VEGETABLES	SAVOURY RICE	FISH	POULTRY & GAME	MEAT	FRUITS
ANGELICA		✓									STEWED
BASIL		TOMATOES	✓	MILK	OMELETTES	MUSHROOMS		FRIED	SHEPHERDS PIE ✓	STEWS	
BAY	✓	✓	✓	MILK		CAULIFLOWER	✓	✓		STEWS	
BORAGE		✓	✓								
BURNET		✓		MILK				✓			
CARAWAY						CABBAGE / TURNIPS				ROAST PORK	
CHERVIL		✓	✓	CREAM / EGG	✓	POTATOES / CARROTS	✓				
CHIVES		✓	✓		✓	POTATOES		✓			
CORIANDER			✓			RICE			CURRIES	CURRIES / STEWS	
DILL		CUCUMBER / DRESSINGS	✓	TOMATO ✓	SCRAMBLED	POTATOES		✓		STEWS	
FENNEL		✓	FISH		✓	YOUNG VEG.		SALMON / MACKEREL	CHICKEN	PORK / VEAL	APPLE PIE
JUNIPER	✓										
GARLIC	✓	✓	✓	✓		CABBAGE		✓	✓	✓	
LOVAGE	✓	✓	VEG ✓	CREAM		✓		✓	✓	STEWS	
MARJORAM		TOMATOES / DRESSINGS			OMELETTES	✓		✓	STUFFING	✓	
MINT			VEG / TOMATO	✓	OMELETTES	POTATOES / PEAS	✓	✓	RABBIT	LAMB	FRUIT SALAD
OREGANO		DRESSINGS			OMELETTES	✓			STUFFING	STEAK	STEWED
PARSLEY	✓	DRESSINGS	✓	CREAM	OMELETTES	✓		✓	STUFFING	LAMB / STEWS	
ROSEMARY				TOMATO				✓	CHICKEN	PORK / LAMB	
SAGE		✓	VEG ✓		OMELETTES	TOMATOES		OILY FISH	GOOSE / DUCK	PORK	
SORREL		✓									
SWEET CICELY											STEWED
TARRAGON		TOMATOES / DRESSINGS	✓	CREAM / EGG	✓	✓	✓	SHELLFISH	✓	VEAL	
THYME	✓	✓	✓	CREAM / TOMATO	BAKED EGG GRATIN	✓	✓	✓	STUFFING / RABBIT	STUFFING	

PLANT FLOWERING TIMES

The plants listed here are those mentioned in the *Wild Plant Reference Section*.
Precise periods when plants are in flower will depend on seasonal variations and
particular local conditions. The '*' indicates possible medical problems and hazards.

	J	F	M	A	M	J	J	A	S	O	N	D
ALEXANDERS				•	•	•	V	V				
WILD ANGELICA*							•	•	•			
ARROWHEAD						•	•	•				
ASH				•	•							
MTN. ASH / ROWAN					•	•						
BARBERRY						•	•		V	V		
BEECHES				•	•				V	V		
BELLFLOWERS						•	•	•	•			
BIRCH				•	•							
BISTORT						•	•	•				
BLADDER CAMPION						•	•	•	•	•		
BORAGE						•	•	•	•	•		
BROOKLIME*						•	•	•	•			
BROOM*						•	•					
BUCKWHEAT							•	•	•			
VIPER'S BUGLOSS						•	•	•	•			
BURDOCK							•	•				
GREAT BURNET						•	•	•	•			
SALAD BURNET					•	•						
BUTCHER'S BROOM*	•	•	•	•								
CARAWAY*					•	•	•	•				
CATMINT							•	•	•			
CATSEAR					•	•	•	•	•			
WILD CELERY						•	•	•				
CHARLOCK/WILD MUSTARD/FIELD MUSTARD			•	•	•	•						
CHICKWEED		•	•	•	•	•	•	•	•			
WILD CHICORY* / SUCCORY							•	•	•			
RED CLOVER					•	•	•	•	•			
COMMON CORNSALAD / LAMB'S LETTUCE				•	•							
CORN SPURREY						•	•	•	•	•		
COSTMARY						•	•					
COUCH GRASS						•	•					
COWSLIP*				•	•							
CUCKOOPINT*				•	•							
COMMON DAISY			•	•	•	•	•	•	•	•		
COMMON DANDELION*			•	•	•	•	•	•	•			
DEAD NETTLE - *L. album*					•	•	•	•	•	•		
- *L. purpuream & amplexicaule*			•	•	•							
BROAD / COMMON DOCK						•	•	•				

	J	F	M	A	M	J	J	A	S	O	N	D
CURLED / SOUR / YELLOW DOCK*				•	•	•						
ELCAMPANE							•	•				
ELDER						•	•					
EVENING PRIMROSE						•	•	•	•			
FAT-HEN / GOOSEFOOT / LAMB'S QUARTERS							•	•	•	•		
WILD FENNEL*							•	•	•	•		
FIELD GARLIC - *A. oleraceum*							•	•				
FLOWERING RUSH							•	•	•			
GOAT'S RUE						•	•					
GOOD KING HENRY				•	•	•	•	•	•	•		
GOOSEGRASS / CLEAVERS						•	•	•	•	•		
GROUND-ELDER / GOUTWEED					•	•	•	•				
GROUND IVY / ALE-HOOF							•	•	•			
GUELDER ROSE / CRANBERRY TREE*				•	•	•						
HAIRY BITTERCRESS				•	•							
HAWTHORN				•	•							
HAWKBITS / HAWKWEEDS							•	•	•	•		
HAZELNUT	•	•	•						∇	∇		
HERB BENNETT / WOOD AVENS						•	•	•				
HOGWEED / COW PARSNIP*					•	•	•	•	•	•		
HOP						•	•	•	•			
HORSERADISH*						•	•	•	•			
HOUSELEEK							•	•				
JAPANESE KNOTWEED								•	•	•		
JUNIPER* [fruits in 2-3 yrs]				•	•	•						
LADY'S SMOCK / CUCKOOFLOWER				•	•	•						
LOVAGE* – *Levisticium officinale*							•	•				
SCOTS LOVAGE* – *Ligusticum scoticum*							•	•	•			
LIME							•	∇	∇	∇		
LUCERNE / ALFALFA							•	•				
COMMON MALLOW*							•	•	•	•	•	•
REED MANNA GRASS				•	•	•	•	•				
REFLEXED MANNA GRASS						•	•	•	•	•		
MARSH MALLOW							•	•	•			
MARSH MARIGOLD*			•	•	•							
MARSH WOUNDWORT							•	•	•			
MEADOWSWEET						•	•	•				
COMMON MELILOT / YLW SWEET CLOVER*					•	•	•	•	•			
MINT – *Mentha piperita* Peppermint								•	•	•		
Mentha aquatica Water mint*							•	•	•	•		
Mentha spicata Spearmint								•	•			
MUGWORT							•	•	•			
BLACK MUSTARD*						•	•	•	•			
GARLIC MUSTARD / HEDGE GARLIC				•	•	•						

	J	F	M	A	M	J	J	A	S	O	N	D
COMMON HEDGE MUSTARD*					•	•	•	•	•			
WHITE MUSTARD						•	•	•	•			
COMMON NETTLE*						•	•	•	•	•		
NIPPLEWORT						•	•	•				
ENGLISH OAK				•	•				V	V		
WILD ONION - *A. vineale*						•	•					
OX-EYE DAISY						•	•					
BRISTLY OX-TONGUE						•	•	•	•	•		
OYSTERPLANT						•	•	•				
COW PARSLEY*				•	•	•	•	•				
WILD PARSNIP*							•	•	•			
PARSLEY PIERT				•	•	•	•	•	•			
FIELD PENNYCRESS				•	•	•						
PIG NUT						•	•					
PLANTAIN - *P. major*						•	•	•	•	•	•	
- *P. lanceolata*						•	•	•	•	•		
COMMON RED POPPY				•	•	•						
PRIMROSE*		•	•	•	•							
WILD RADISH				•	•	•	•	•				
RAMSONS				•								
RAPE*				•	•	•	•					
COMMON REED							•	•	•			
REEDMACE / CAT'S-TAIL						•	•	•				
COMMON REST-HARROW / WILD LIQUORICE						•	•	•	•			
ROSEBAY WILLOWHERB*						•	•	•	•			
COMMON SCURVYGRASS					•	•	•	•				
SEA-KALE						•	•	•				
SELF HEAL						•	•	•	•	•		
SHEPHERD'S PURSE		•	•	•	•	•	•	•	•	•	•	
SILVERWEED						•	•	•	•			
SNEEZEWORT						•	•	•	•	•		
PRICKLY SOW-THISTLE						•	•	•	•	•		
SMOOTH SOW-THISTLE						•	•	•	•	•		
CORN / PERENNIAL SOW-THISTLE						•	•	•	•	•		
SHEEP'S SORREL					•	•	•					
WILD / COMMON SORREL*					•	•	•	•				
WOOD SORREL*			•	•	•							
SPIGNEL						•	•					
SPRING BEAUTIES			•	•	•	•						
STAR OF BETHLEHEM*				•	•	•						
STORK'S BILL				•	•	•	•					
SWEET CICELY					•	•	•					
SWEET SEDGE / SWEET FLAG					•	•	•					
SYCAMORE / GREAT MAPLE				•	•	V	V	V	V			

	J	F	M	A	M	J	J	A	S	O	N	D
MILK THISTLE / WILD ARTICHOKE*						•	•	•				
THISTLE* - *C. vulgare*						•	•	•	•			
COTTON THISTLE						•	•	•				
WOOLLY THISTLE						•	•	•				
RED VALERIAN						•	•	•				
BITTER VETCH*			•	•	•	•						
VIOLET - *V. odorata*		•	•									
V. riviniana			•	•								
WALL LETTUCE							•	•	•			
WATER AVENS						•	•	•				
COMMON WATERCRESS*						•	•	•				
WATER CROWFOOT					•	•						
WATER LILY – *Nymphaea alba*						•	•	•				
WILD SERVICE TREE					•	•			∇			
WHITEBEAM					•	•			∇			
WHORTLEBERRY / BILBERRY - *V. myrtillus*				•	•	•						
- *V. vitis-idaea*						•	•					
WILLOW – *S. alba*				•	•							
WINTER CRESS						•	•	•	•			
YARROW / MILFOIL*						•	•	•	•	•		
YELLOW / MEADOW GOAT'S BEARD						•	•					
COMMON YEW*		•	•	•				∇	∇			

When trying one of the wild plants listed for the first time, try tasting just a small amount of the prepared plant to check your tolerance. If you have any bad or allergic reactions avoid any further consumption.

Never put any plant into your mouth unless absolutely 100% certain of its identification and edibility. Don't even consider 'pretty sure' as an option.

Only gather ingredients from uncontaminated sources and environments.

PLANT FLOWERING TIME BY MONTH

The plants listed here are those mentioned in the *Wild Plant Reference Section*. Precise periods when plants are in flower will depend on seasonal variations and particular local conditions. The '*' indicates possible medical problems and hazards.

	J	F	M	A	M	J	J	A	S	O	N	D
HAZELNUT	•	•	•						V	V		
BUTCHER'S BROOM*	•	•	•	•								
COMMON YEW*		•	•	•				V	V			
PRIMROSE*		•	•	•	•							
SHEPHERD'S PURSE		•	•	•	•	•	•	•	•	•	•	
VIOLET – *V. odorata*			•	•								
DEAD NETTLES - *L. purpuream/amplexicaule*			•	•	•							
MARSH MARIGOLD*			•	•	•							
WOOD SORREL*			•	•	•							
CHARLOCK / WILD MUSTARD			•	•	•	•						
SPRING BEAUTIES			•	•	•	•						
COMMON DANDELION*			•	•	•	•	•	•				
CHICKWEED			•	•	•	•	•	•	•	•		
COMMON DAISY			•	•	•	•	•	•	•	•		
DEAD NETTLES - *L. album*				•	•	•	•	•	•	•		
GOOD KING HENRY				•	•	•	•	•	•	•		
ASH				•	•							
BIRCH				•	•							
COMMON CORNSALAD / LAMB'S LETTUCE				•	•							
COWSLIP*				•	•							
CUCKOOPINT*				•	•							
VIOLET – *V. riviniana*				•	•							
WILLOW – *S. alba*				•	•							
SYCAMORE / GREAT MAPLE				•	•	V	V	V	V			
BEECHES				•	•				V	V		
ENGLISH OAK				•	•				V	V		
ALEXANDERS				•	•	•						
FIELD PENNYCRESS				•	•	•						
GARLIC MUSTARD / HEDGE GARLIC				•	•	•						
JUNIPER* [fruits after 2-3 years]				•	•	•						
LADY'S SMOCK / CUCKOOFLOWER				•	•	•						
STAR OF BETHLEHEM*				•	•	•						
WHORTLEBERRY / BILBERRY - *V. myrtillus*				•	•	•						
CARAWAY*				•	•	•	•					
STORK'S BILL				•	•	•	•					
BITTER VETCH*				•	•	•	•					
COW PARSLEY*				•	•	•	•	•				

	J	F	M	A	M	J	J	A	S	O	N	D
REED MANNA GRASS				•	•	•	•	•				
PARSLEY PIERT				•	•	•	•	•	•	•		
RAMSONS				•								
BROOM*					•	•						
HAIRY BITTERCRESS					•	•						
HAWTHORN					•	•						
MTN. ASH / ROWAN					•	•						
PIG NUT					•	•						
SALAD BURNET					•	•						
WATER CROWFOOT					•	•						
WHITEBEAM					•	•			∇			
WILD SERVICE TREE					•	•			∇			
BARBERRY					•	•			∇	∇		
ARROWHEAD					•	•	•					
BISTORT					•	•	•					
COMMON RED POPPY					•	•	•					
CURLED / SOUR / YELLOW DOCK*					•	•	•					
GUELDER ROSE / CRANBERRY TREE*					•	•	•					
SHEEP'S SORREL*					•	•	•					
SWEET CICELY					•	•	•					
SWEET SEDGE / SWEET FLAG					•	•	•					
BROOKLIME*					•	•	•	•				
COMMON SCURVYGRASS					•	•	•	•				
GROUND-ELDER / GOUTWEED					•	•	•	•				
HOP					•	•	•	•				
HORSERADISH*					•	•	•	•				
RAPE*					•	•	•	•				
SILVERWEED					•	•	•	•				
WILD / COMMON SORREL*					•	•	•	•				
WINTER CRESS					•	•	•	•				
BLADDER CAMPION					•	•	•	•	•			
BORAGE					•	•	•	•	•			
CATSEAR					•	•	•	•	•			
RED CLOVER					•	•	•	•	•			
COMMON HEDGE MUSTARD*					•	•	•	•	•			
COMMON MELILOT / YLW SWEET CLOVER*					•	•	•	•	•			
WILD RADISH					•	•	•	•	•			
HOGWEED / COW PARSNIP*					•	•	•	•	•	•		
SELF HEAL					•	•	•	•	•	•		
PLANTAIN - *P. major*					•	•	•	•	•	•	•	
COSTMARY						•	•					
COUCH GRASS						•	•					
ELDERBERRY						•	•					
GOAT'S RUE						•	•					

	J	F	M	A	M	J	J	A	S	O	N	D
HOUSELEEK						•	•					
LUCERNE / ALFALFA						•	•					
WILD ONION – A. *vineale*						•	•					
OX-EYE DAISY						•	•					
SPIGNEL						•	•					
WHORTLEBERRY - V. *vitis-idaea*						•	•					
YELLOW / MEADOW GOAT'S BEARD						•	•					
WILD CELERY						•	•	•				
BROAD / COMMON DOCK						•	•	•				
HERB BENNET / WOOD AVENS						•	•	•				
SCOTS LOVAGE* – *Ligusticum scoticum*						•	•	•				
MEADOWSWEET						•	•	•				
NIPPLEWORT						•	•	•				
OYSTERPLANT						•	•	•				
REEDMACE / CAT'S-TAIL						•	•	•				
SEA-KALE						•	•	•				
MILK THISTLE / WILD ARTICHOKE						•	•	•				
RED VALERIAN						•	•	•				
WATER AVENS						•	•	•				
COMMON WATERCRESS*						•	•	•				
WATER LILY – *Nymphaea alba*						•	•	•				
BELLFLOWERS						•	•	•	•			
VIPER'S BUGLOSS						•	•	•	•			
GREAT BURNET						•	•	•	•			
HAWKBITS / HAWKWEEDS						•	•	•	•			
EVENING PRIMROSE						•	•	•	•			
BLACK MUSTARD*						•	•	•	•			
WHITE MUSTARD						•	•	•	•			
COMMON REST-HARROW						•	•	•	•			
ROSEBAY WILLOWHERB*						•	•	•	•			
CORN SPURREY						•	•	•	•	•		
GOOSEGRASS / CLEAVERS						•	•	•	•	•		
REFLEXED MANNA GRASS						•	•	•	•	•		
BRISTLY OX-TONGUE						•	•	•	•	•		
COMMON NETTLE						•	•	•	•	•		
PLANTAIN - P. *lanceolata*						•	•	•	•	•		
SNEEZEWORT						•	•	•	•	•		
PRICKLY SOW-THISTLE						•	•	•	•	•		
SMOOTH SOW-THISTLE						•	•	•	•	•		
CORN / PERENNIAL SOW-THISTLE						•	•	•	•	•		
YARROW / MILFOIL*						•	•	•	•	•		
COMMON MALLOW*						•	•	•	•	•	•	
LIME							•	V	V	V		
BURDOCK						•	•					

	J	F	M	A	M	J	J	A	S	O	N	D
ELCAMPANE							•	•				
FIELD GARLIC - *A. oleraceum*							•	•				
LOVAGE* – *Levisticium officinale*							•	•				
WILD ANGELICA*							•	•	•			
BUCKWHEAT							•	•	•			
CATMINT							•	•	•			
WILD CHICORY* / SUCCORY							•	•	•			
FLOWERING RUSH							•	•	•			
GROUND IVY / ALE-HOOF							•	•	•			
WALL LETTUCE							•	•	•			
MARSH MALLOW							•	•	•			
MARSH WOUNDWORT							•	•	•			
MUGWORT							•	•	•			
WILD PARSNIP*							•	•	•			
COMMON REED							•	•	•			
COTTON THISTLE							•	•	•			
WOOLLY THISTLE							•	•	•			
FAT-HEN / LAMB'S QUARTERS							•	•	•	•		
WILD FENNEL							•	•	•	•		
MINT – *Mentha aquatica* Water*							•	•	•	•		
THISTLE* - *C. vulgare*							•	•	•	•		
MINT – *Mentha spicata* Spearmint								•	•			
JAPANESE KNOTWEED								•	•	•		
MINT – *Mentha piperita* Peppermint								•	•	•		

When trying one of the wild plants listed for the first time, try tasting just a small amount of the prepared plant to check your tolerance. If you have any bad or allergic reactions avoid any further consumption.

Never put any plant into your mouth unless absolutely 100% certain of its identification and edibility. Don't even consider 'pretty sure' as an option.

Only gather ingredients from uncontaminated sources and environments.

INDEX